Intersectionality for Social Workers

CW01500389

This book explores how intersectionality theory can be applied to social work practice with children and families, older people and mental health service users, and used to engage with diversity and difference in social work education and research.

With case-study examples and practice questions throughout, the book provides a model for integrating intersectionality theory into social work practice. It highlights the ways intersectional theory helps us to understand the complexities of working with the interlocking nature of problematised elements such as gender, race, class, sexuality, disability, and other axes of structural inequalities experienced by groups in subjugated social locations. Intersectionality is used to examine multiple forms of inequalities and the complexities and questions they give rise to in social work practice. The emphasis throughout is that intersectional approaches can open up social work practice to new understandings of the complex linkages of multiple and intersecting systems of oppression that shape the lived experiences of diverse groups of service users.

Providing an introduction to an intersectional theoretical framework for understanding the lives and experiences of socially disadvantaged service users, *Intersectionality for Social Workers* will be required reading on all modules on anti-oppressive and anti-discriminatory practice, sociology, and ethics and values in social work.

Claudia Bernard is Professor of Social Work in the Department of Social, Therapeutic and Community Studies at Goldsmiths, University of London, UK.

Intersectionality for Social Workers

A Practical Introduction to Theory and Practice

Claudia Bernard

Routledge
Taylor & Francis Group

LONDON AND NEW YORK

First published 2022
by Routledge
2 Park Square, Milton Park, Abingdon, Oxon OX14 4RN

and by Routledge
605 Third Avenue, New York, NY 10158

Routledge is an imprint of the Taylor & Francis Group, an informa business

© 2022 Claudia Bernard

The right of Claudia Bernard to be identified as author of this work has been asserted by her in accordance with sections 77 and 78 of the Copyright, Designs and Patents Act 1988.

All rights reserved. No part of this book may be reprinted or reproduced or utilised in any form or by any electronic, mechanical, or other means, now known or hereafter invented, including photocopying and recording, or in any information storage or retrieval system, without permission in writing from the publishers.

Trademark notice: Product or corporate names may be trademarks or registered trademarks, and are used only for identification and explanation without intent to infringe.

British Library Cataloguing-in-Publication Data
A catalogue record for this book is available from the British Library

Library of Congress Cataloging-in-Publication Data
Names: Bernard, Claudia, author.
Title: Intersectionality for social workers : a practical introduction to theory and practice / Claudia Bernard.
Description: New York, NY : Routledge, 2022. | Includes bibliographical references and index.
Subjects: LCSH: Intersectionality (Sociology) | Social service.
Classification: LCC HM488.5 .B47 2022 (print) | LCC HM488.5 (ebook) | DDC 305—dc23
LC record available at https://lccn.loc.gov/2021028752
LC ebook record available at https://lccn.loc.gov/2021028753

ISBN: 978-1-138-60719-4 (hbk)
ISBN: 978-1-138-60721-7 (pbk)
ISBN: 978-0-429-46728-8 (ebk)

DOI: 10.4324/9780429467288

Typeset in Helvetica
by Apex CoVantage, LLC

Contents

Acknowledgements

Writing this book would not have been possible without the support of a number of people. I owe a debt of gratitude to all the fantastic students, practitioners, and managers that I have dialogued with over the years, whose knowledge and ideas have enhanced my thinking and understanding about social work practice. Thanks also to my colleagues in the Department of Social, Therapeutic and Community Studies at Goldsmiths, for facilitating an environment conducive to my writing. I am appreciative of Sharon Jennings, Anna Fairtlough, and Joan Fletcher for providing thoughtful feedback on the chapter on social work education. A special word of thanks to Professor Frank Keating, Royal Holloway, University of London, for sharing some of his insights about mental health social work. I extend my appreciation to Carline Benoit, Michaela Dunn, Susan Hasler-Winter, and Carol Roberts who went out of their way to enable me to have access to practice examples and have been very supportive in sharing their knowledge about child and family social work. I want to thank my dear friends Khalida Khan and Jacqui Beckford for their enthusiasm, friendship, and encouragement throughout. Thanks as well to my dear sister, Heather Bernard, for her love and support. A very special thanks goes to my editor at Routledge, Clair Jarvis, for inviting me to write this book and for her commitment to the project; she has been very patient and supportive in working with me towards the book's conclusion. I also must acknowledge the work of Catherine Jones for guiding the book through production. Finally, special thanks to my partner David Katz, for his love and support throughout the writing of this book.

Foreword

Covid-19 has shone a light on the many inequalities that scar our society. As we attempt to understand who has died and why, as well as the differences in living situations for so many others, we are obliged to reflect on the consequences of decades of policy choices that have left so many in such precarious situations, at the mercy of market forces that denied vulnerability and interdependence.

The writer and activist Rebecca Solnit notes that:

> **The first lesson a disaster teaches is that everything is con-nected** … At moments of immense change, we see with new clarity the systems – political, economic, social, ecological – in which we are immersed as they change around us. We see what's strong, what's weak, what's corrupt, what matters and what doesn't. I often think of these times as akin to a spring thaw: it's as if the pack ice has broken up, the water starts flowing again and boats can move through places they could not during winter. The ice was the arrangement of power relations that we call the status quo – it seems to be stable, and those who benefit from it often insist that it's unchangeable. Then it changes fast and dra-matically, and that can be exhilarating, terrifying, or both.
>
> (Solnit, 2020, emphasis added, no page numbers)

The term intersectionality has spoken to attempts to understand how the interconnections operate and, crucially, reveal the power relations that characterise them. For example, how can we come to terms with and understand the following?

> Put differently, we estimate over 58,000 and 35,000 additional deaths from Covid-19 would have occurred if the white population

had experienced the same risk of death from Covid-19 as the Black and South Asian populations respectively.

(IPPR and Runnymede Trust, 2020, no page numbers)

In seeking to understand and eradicate such gross inequalities it has been vital to challenge the inadequacies of a decades-long frame focused solely on the role of individual choices and behaviours in managing and controlling risk. A wider frame has been needed to drill down into why those from Black, Asian, and Minority Ethnic communities were so fatally at risk in this pandemic. This requires making connections between individual choices and public troubles, notably, the systemic racism underpinning occupational arrangements and policies that bake in long-standing health, income, and housing inequalities and the myriad of ways these intersect to reinforce vulnerability and precarity.

Unfortunately, social work has not been immune from the decades-long preoccupation with enforcing individual responsibility for the risks faced by poor and marginalised communities. While this has been a particularly pronounced feature of policy and practice in child protection, no area of social work has escaped unscathed from an individualising logic which has rendered human troubles attributable to individuals' poor choices and risky behaviours.

I am therefore delighted to welcome this timely and important book by Professor Claudia Bernard. It offers vital conceptual and practical insights into how an intersectional theoretical perspective can be used in social work education and practice to understand the constraints and possibilities faced by those seeking to navigate an unequal landscape from differentiated locations.

In highlighting the complexities of working with the interlocking nature of gender, race, class, sexuality, disability, and other axes of structural inequalities, it offers opportunities and challenges for social work. Intersectional approaches open up social work to new understandings of the complex linkages of multiple and intersecting systems of oppression that shape the lived experiences of diverse groups of service users. They offer important opportunities to see the whole person in all their complexity and refuse the seductions of the single story whether that is about a situation or a family.

However, the challenges are considerable going forward. In his book the historian Frank Snowden (2020) examines the ways in which disease outbreaks have shaped politics, crushed revolutions, and entrenched racial and economic discrimination. His work, and that of other historians, provides a necessary corrective to optimistic assumptions that the exposure of so many of society's inequalities and frailties will lead to building back fairer or indeed even better. Indeed, it seems while every disaster is different, they always do bring both loss and gain. And in this pandemic, while Covid-19 highlights our common fate and should reinforce solidarity, the recognition of differential levels of vulnerability has already contributed to stigmatisation and othering.

In this context, Professor Bernard's book is even more important for social work going forward. The pandemic has prompted some reflection on values, ethics, and inequalities and there has been evidence of solidarity and care in terms of practice responses. This book has the potential to ensure these are sustained as part of a society-wide project to build back fairer and better.

Professor Brid Featherstone, University of Huddersfield

References

IPPR and Runnymede Trust 2020. Ethnic inequalities in Covid-19 are playing out again – how can we stop them? Available at: www.ippr.org/blog/ethnic-inequalities-in-covid-19-are-playing-out-again-how-can-we-stop-them.

Snowden, F. 2020. *Epidemics and Society: From the Black Death to the Present.* London: Yale University Press.

Solnit, R. 2020. The impossible has already happened. Available at: www.theguardian.com/world/2020/apr/07/what-coronavirus-can-teach-us-about-hope-rebecca-solnit.

1 Introduction

This book explores how an intersectional theoretical perspective can be used in social work education and practice to engage with diversity and difference. It highlights the contributions that intersectional theory can make to help us understand the complexities of working with the interlocking nature of problematised elements such as gender, race, class, sexuality, disability, and other axes of structural inequalities experienced by groups in subjugated social locations. Intersectionality is used as a means to examine multiple forms of inequalities and the complexities and questions they give rise to in social work practice. The emphasis throughout is that intersectional approaches can open up social work practice to new understandings of the complex linkages of multiple and intersecting systems of oppression that shape the lived experiences of diverse groups of service users. Central to an intersectional perspective is its capacity for developing alternative epistemologies to make us think in new ways about how the oppressed and discriminated against are impacted by the overlapping nature of forms of oppression in their particular social contexts (Hill Collins 1990; Yuval-Davis 2006a; Yuval-Davis 2006b). An important feature of an intersectional approach to social work is that it offers an alternative lens through which to examine how contexts of oppression underlie the social problems that social workers have to respond to in welfare interventions (Murphy et al. 2009). My goal in this book is to therefore provide a basic introduction of an intersectional theoretical framework for understanding the lives and experiences of socially disadvantaged service users.

In this introductory chapter, I set the scene by laying out the broad scope of the text. Opening with a brief outline of key terms and concepts, it will provide an overview of the range of issues that will be discussed and will also detail the common themes running through the book, namely the use of intersectionality and anti-oppressive

DOI: 10.4324/9780429467288-1

practice in social work. In particular, this introductory chapter will articulate some of the key themes and practice issues in social work to illuminate how the book will offer relevant insights.

Intersectionality

Intersectionality, a term first coined by Kimberlé Crenshaw (Crenshaw 1989; 1991), is a theoretical tool with its roots firmly anchored in black feminist thought and critical race theory that has primarily sought to interrogate the interacting layers of various systems of oppression that affect the lived experiences of black women. The central tenet of an intersectional theoretical perspective is that it provides the analytical tools to conceptualise how multiple categories of difference intersect and interplay in a context of social relations of power, which advances understanding of how divergent groups may experience oppression differently. A number of intersectional feminist scholars from a range of disciplines have elaborated the ways in which intersectionality is key to analysing multiple social categories of race, gender, class, sexuality, religion, nationality, age, disability, and other markers of identity interplay to structure the relational and contextual nature of black women's lived experiences (Alexander-Floyd and Nikol 2012; Anthias 2001; Brah and Phoenix 2004; Hill Collins 1990; hooks 1984; King 1988; Lewis 2013; Rodgers 2017). According to Yuval-Davis (2006a), intersectionality allows for the examination of the interlocking nature of gender, race, class, sexuality, disability, and other social divisions for marginalised groups in oppressed social locations. In recent years the language of intersectionality is now widely used by scholars, researchers, and activists in different fields and disciplines as an organising and political tool to identify and call into question social inequities and analyses of difference (Bilge 2013; Emejulu and Mügge 2018; Hill Collins 2015; Hill Collins and Bilge 2016; Jordan-Zachery 2007; Kantola and Nousiainen 2009; Kanyeredzi 2018; McCall 2005; Mehrotra 2010; Mirza 2015; Nayak and Robbins 2018; Prins 2006; Yuval-Davis 2006b).

Why a book about intersectionality and social work?

In the field of social work, there is a growing body of literature using intersectionality as a framework to harness the values of social justice and human rights perspectives, thus a number of scholars have applied intersectionality to a wide range of practice, policy, and research debates (Barretti 2015; Bubar et al. 2016; Busche et al. 2012; Fong 2004; Gunn et al. 2016; Hicks 2015 Mantovani and Thomas 2014; Mattsson 2014; Mehrotra 2010; Murphy et al. 2009; Nayak and Robbins 2018). In particular, critical race scholars have used an intersectionality orientation to underscore the importance of race in social work and, most importantly, for probing the multidimensional facets of marginalised racial, ethnic, and religious groups' experience of social work (Badwall 2016; Barn and Sidhu 2004; Bernard 2019; Bhatti-Sinclair 2011; Bhui 2002; Dalrymple and Burke 2006; Dominelli 1988; Lavelette and Penketh 2014; Okitikpi and Aymer 2010; Robinson et al. 2011; Williams 1999; Williams and Johnson 2010). Feminist scholars in social work have drawn on the explanatory power of intersectionality for elucidating the gender aspects that underlie much social work practice with families and especially to foreground the mother-blaming discourses that pervade much of social work thinking and practice (Bernard 2013; Davis and Gentlewarrior 2015; Dominelli and McLeod 1989; Turner and Maschi 2015; Krumer-Nevo and Komem 2015; Wendt and Moulding 2017).

This book emerges from the increasing recognition that there is a need for perspectives that can provide insight into how sources of oppression interact for a nuanced understanding of the diversity of issues that social workers have to grapple with. Because of demographic changes, the UK population has become more racially, ethnically, and religiously diverse, so it has become imperative that social workers are able to understand the complexity of the lived experiences of the individuals, groups, and communities they work with. Most notably, this racially and culturally diverse population includes families and groups of varying races and ethnicities who have recently migrated from different countries in Africa and Asia, and second and third generation British-born children of Caribbean, African, and Asian descent (many of whom are of mixed heritage), as well as newly arrived migrants from sub-Saharan Africa, Syria, Afghanistan, and Iraq, among other places. It should also be noted that in Britain, 'Muslims belong to a diverse range of ethnic and national groups, including Afghan, Arab, Iranian, Indian, Kosovan, Kurdish, Turkish and Somalian communities' (Garland et al. 2006, 427). It is certainly the case that diversity issues are much more complex and multifaceted as migrants come from more diverse national, ethnic, linguistic, and religious backgrounds, have more varied legal statuses, and bring a wide array of human capital in terms of education, work skills, and experience (Boccagni 2015; Foner et al. 2017; Geldof 2016; Van Robaeys et al. 2018). To be sure, because of the heterogeneity of the minority ethnic groups, their needs will be highly differentiated, resulting most notably in a highly complex range of social work issues to address in contemporary practice. What is more important, however, is that with the increasing demographic diversity of service users in the UK, the challenges that social workers have to confront in practice in making complex decisions with significant legal, ethical, and value-based dimensions have become much more complicated. As Williams and Mikola (2018) point out, with the diverse demographics of racial minorities there are significant challenges for social work practice.

In various domains of social work, a number of key scholars have used intersectionality to draw attention to the ways in which mutually reinforcing systems of structural and situational inequalities impact service users' experiences of social work and, above all, the way that needs and problems are conceptualised for black and minority ethnic groups. A case in point is in the field of child and family social work where there has been growing attention paid to emergent forms of abuse and harmful behaviours that call into question different child-rearing practices. For example, abuse linked to faith and beliefs, such as FGM, honour-based violence, and forced marriage (Costello et al. 2015; Gupta, 2016); witchcraft or spirit possession (Briggs et al. 2011; DfE 2012; Tedam 2016; Tedam and Adjoa 2017); gang-associated physical and sexual violence (Beckett et al. 2013; Firmin 2018; Pearce 2014; Pitts 2013); human trafficking or sexual exploitation (Stobart 2006; Bokhari 2008); and unaccompanied minors at risk of human rights violations (Westwood 2016) to name but a few. In other practice settings, scholars employing tenets of intersectionality have explored mental health debates (Barn 2008; Fernando 2003; Fernando and Keating 2009; Keating 2016); to articulate emancipatory approaches to study disability (Campbell 2014; Carr 2014); to stimulate debates about older people, ageing and the life course perspectives (Chaney 2011; Calasanti and King 2015; Cuesta and Rämgård 2016; Duffy 2017; King et al. 2019; Hafford-Letchfield 2013; Rajan-Rankin 2018; Torres 2019; Wilkens 2019). Additionally, it is now increasingly recognised by scholars that social workers must acknowledge the significance of the role of faith, spirituality, and religion for black and minority ethnic groups accessing social work support (Crisp 2017; Dinham 2018; Hodge 2017; Holloway and Moss 2010; Furness and Gillian 2014; Pentaris 2012).

What becomes clear is that the complex multidimensional issues affecting diverse populations result in social workers delivering services to a much broader range of service users than previously. Thus, put simply, we can see the increased relevance of intersectionality perspectives for social work particularly at a theoretical, methodological, and practice level. In other words, there is a need for theoretical frameworks like intersectionality that can help disentangle the interplay of the multiplicity of injustices borne of inequalities that bring minority groups and families from diverse racial and cultural backgrounds into the social welfare system in the UK. Intersectionality thus has the potential to enrich social work theory and practice and this book will therefore offer a new angle on an important theoretical perspective to social work in the UK. Perhaps more importantly, intersectionality allows us to delineate the contextual, social, and environmental factors that affect service users' lives and offers a framework for developing strengths-based practice. While this book refers to and references the body of work being undertaken internationally, its focus is on the way that intersectionality can inform social work practice in the UK.

Overview of the book

The book is organised in three sections. The first traces the historical development of intersectionality theory to consider its relevance for contemporary social work in the UK. The second explores applications of intersectionality theory for social work interventions in different practice situations, with chapters focusing on children and families, adult services, and mental health. The final section focuses on social work education to consider the teaching and learning of intersectional theory and its utility as an analytical tool in social work research. A key feature of the book is its blending of theory, case studies, reflective questions, and chapter summary questions, to illustrate how an intersectional perspective can be applied to interventions grounded in social justice values and principles.

The book is made up of eight chapters. In Chapter 2, I begin by mapping an historical overview of intersectionality, to trace its development from critical race feminism, and its particular use by US scholars, to provide a contextual backdrop for the theory. The chapter will discuss the emergence of the term intersectionality and summarises the core tenets of the theory. It will also set out the different perspectives of intersectionality and consider the competing ideas as to whether it is a theory, a framework, a model, a method, a metaphor, or a paradigm. Additionally, this chapter looks at feminist critiques of intersectionality. The criticism often levelled at intersectionality is of its open-ended nature; thus, it is often misapplied or misunderstood or dismissed as too abstract. Therefore, as well as outlining some of the perspectives of intersectionality, critiques of intersectionality will also be summarised here, to highlight why the theory was created and to delineate what it is and is not. In this chapter, I will also provide a review of the literature on the development of intersectional approaches to social work. Here the emphasis is on drawing attention to the contribution of intersectional perspectives to the knowledge base for social work and tracing the implications of the theory for praxis and education. Although the past few years have seen an upsurge of articles addressing intersectionality in different areas of social work practice, much of this originates in North America (e.g., Bubar et al. 2016; Busche et al. 2012; Mattsson 2014; Murphy et al. 2009; Robinson et al. 2011). There has been less scholarly attention given to intersectionality in the UK, and when intersectional ideas are considered in British social work, it is often within anti-discriminatory and anti-oppressive practice debates about the interconnected dynamics of power, oppression, and privilege. Thus, the main goal of this chapter is to draw out how intersectionality theorising opens up new areas and frameworks for investigations of the contextual factors that frame services users' encounters with social work services in the UK.

Chapter 3 examines how intersectionality can be applied in work with children and families in situations of child abuse and neglect. With a particular focus on interventions with children in the child protection system, this chapter will link theory to practice by utilising case examples to show how an intersectionality approach can be used to make sense of risk and protective factors for children in danger of harm. The aim here is to show how the theoretical model can be used as an organising tool in assessments of the children's development needs, as well as parenting capacity and family and environmental factors when there are safeguarding concerns. The main argument of the chapter is that using intersectionality as an organising framework can help foster understandings of the barriers and facilitators to parental engagement in a context where there is heterogeneity of parenting styles and different cultural norms concerning child-rearing. Case examples will be used to illustrate different categories of abuse, including physical abuse, neglect, sexual abuse, and the effects of domestic abuse.

The focus of Chapter 4 is on how the tools of intersectionality can be used in mental health social work. The main argument in the chapter is that attempts by mental health social workers to empower service users/survivors in the social welfare system must engage with the socio-cultural context of their lives. Using intersectionality as a prism, the chapter will explore how mental health users' multiple identities and interlocking systemic inequalities interact to underpin the contextual factors for racialised groups in the mental health system. The complex interface between the Mental Health Act and the Mental Capacity Act will be considered to analyse best interest decision-making processes. With the use of case studies, the chapter will show how an intersectional approach can help develop critical understanding of how issues of race, gender, and class interplay with discourses of 'risk' and 'dangerousness' in mental health.

In doing so, the chapter will use intersectionality to interrogate key principles and values that underpin policy and practice, as well as the organisational issues and their impact on social work roles and relationships with mental health service users. The suggestion is made in the chapter that, as social workers in the mental health field must work across professional boundaries, an intersectional approach will extend knowledge of multidisciplinary work, inter-agency partnerships and partnership working with service users and carers.

In Chapter 5, the focus is on social work with older people, defined here as aged 65 years and over. Focusing on themes of empowerment, participation, and personalisation, the chapter will use an intersectionality lens of analysis to examine the policy and organisational context of social work with older people, as well as the skills, knowledge, and values necessary for this area of practice. Using different case scenarios, the chapter will show how an intersectional approach can help navigate the multiple intersections of oppression for older people with diverse needs.

Chapter 6 addresses how intersectional approaches can be used as a pedagogical tool to teach about a range of topics in social work. Providing a critical framework for understanding multiple categories of oppression, the chapter will look at how intersectionality can be used as an analytical tool to develop critical thinking skills in social work education. The core themes of intersectionality, such as power, relationality, social inequality, complexity, social context, and social justice will be expounded on to show that they can be used in learning and teaching (Hill Collins and Bilge 2016). In particular, the chapter will explore how social work scholars and practice educators may use an intersectional framework to ask different kinds of questions and facilitate deeper conversations about the intersections of multiple forms of oppression that structure the experiences of service users' identities and subjectivities in their everyday lives. The chapter will also provide examples of the pedagogical strategies that can be used in the classroom setting and practice-learning environment in the teaching of students for self-awareness and skills development, and especially for addressing difficult and emotionally charged topics such as racism, religious beliefs, or homophobia.

Chapter 7 is concerned with how an intersectionality perspective can be used in the teaching of research methods for doing social work research. The main argument in this chapter is that it is critical for students to have good research skills and to understand research approaches, as well as for practitioners to be research-minded for evidence-based practice (Humphries 2008; Windsong 2018). With a particular focus on interventions with children at risk of abuse and neglect, this chapter will link theory to practice by utilising case examples to show how an intersectional approach can be used not only to read and understand research, but also to actually undertake original research. The chapter will use the key principles of intersectionality to help students understand the complexities of practices involved in research; to understand the ethical issues involved in research; to develop their capacity to critically evaluate research findings and their own practice; and to evaluate research drawing on anti-discriminatory and anti-oppressive perspectives. Examples drawn from a wide range of research studies will be used to provide some practical ideas for how an intersectional approach can be utilised in research, including in studies on teenage mothers, neglect in affluent families, black mothers' responses to child sexual abuse, and diversity and progression in social work.

Chapter 8, the concluding chapter, brings together the crucial themes of the book to draw out its key messages for social work education, research, and practice, and ends with some reflections and strategies for social work.

References

Alexander-Floyd, Nikol G. 2012. Disappearing acts: Reclaiming intersectionality in the social sciences in a post-black feminist era. *Feminist Formations* 24 (1): 1–25.

Anthias, Floya. 2001. The material and the symbolic in theorizing social stratification. *British Journal of Sociology* 52 (3): 367–390.

Badwall, Harjeet Kaur. 2016. Racialized discourses: Writing against an essentialized story about racism. *Intersectionalities* 5 (1): 8–19.

Barn, Ravinder. 2008. Ethnicity, gender and mental health: Social worker perspectives. *International Journal of Social Psychiatry* 54 (1): 69–82.

Barn, Ravinder, and Kalwant Sidhum. 2004. Understanding the interconnections between ethnicity, gender, social class and health: Experiences of ethnic minority women in Britain. *Social Work in Health Care* 39 (1–2): 11–27.

Barretti, Marietta A. 2015. In search of women of colour in the social work journal literature (1998–2007). *Affilia* 20 (4): 427–446.

Beckett, Helen, Isabelle Brodie, Fiona Factor, Margaret Melrose, Jenny Pearce, John Pitts, Lucie Shuker, and Camille Warrington. 2013. It's wrong but you get used to it: A qualitative study of gang-associated sexual violence towards, and sexual exploitation of, young people in England. London: Office of the Children's Commissioner.

Bernard, Claudia. 2013. Black feminist thinking, black mothers and child sexual abuse. In *Failure to Protect: Moving Beyond Gendered Responses*, eds. Susan Strega, Julia Krane, Simon Lapierre and Cathy Richardson. Black Point, Nova Scotia: Fernwood Press.

Bernard, Claudia. 2019. Using an intersectional lens to examine the child sexual exploitation of black adolescents. In *Child Sexual Exploitation: Why Theory Matters*, ed. Jenny Pearce, 193–208. Bristol: Policy Press.

Bhatti-Sinclair, Kish. 2011. *Anti-Racist Practice in Social Work*. Basingstoke: Palgrave Macmillan.

Bhui, Kamaldeep. 2002. *Racism in Mental Health: Prejudice and Suffering*. London: Jessica Kingsley.

Bilge, Sirma. 2013. Intersectionality undone: Saving intersectionality from feminist intersectionality studies. *Du Bois Review* 10 (2): 405–424.

Boccagni, Paolo. 2015. (Super)diversity and the migration–social work nexus: A new lens on the field of access and inclusion? *Ethnic and Racial Studies* 38 (4): 608–620.

Bokhari, Farrah. 2008. Falling through the gaps: Safeguarding children trafficked into the UK. *Children and Society* 22, 201–211.

Brah, Avtar, and Ann Phoenix. 2004. Ain't I a woman? Revisiting intersectionality. *Journal of International Women's Studies* 5 (3): 75–86.

Briggs, Stephen, Andrew Whittaker, Hannah Linford, Agnes Bryan, Elaine Ryan and Dawn Ludick. 2011. *Safeguarding Children's Rights: Exploring Issues of Witchcraft and Spirit Possession in London's African Communities.* London: Trust for London.

Bubar, Roe, Karina Cespedes and Kimberly Bundy-Fazioli. 2016. Intersectionality and social work: Omissions of race, class, and sexuality in Graduate School Education. *Journal of Social Work Education* 52 (3): 283–296.

Busche, Mart, Elli Scambor and Olaf Stuve. 2012. An intersectional perspective in social work and education. *ERIS web journal.*

Calasanti, Toni, and Neal King. 2015. Intersectionality and age. In *Routledge Handbook of Cultural Gerontology*, eds. Julia Twigg and Wendy Martin, 193–200. New York: Routledge.

Campbell, Fiona Kumari. 2014. Ableism as transformative practice. In *Rethinking Anti-Discriminatory and Anti-Oppressive Theories for Social Work Practice,* eds. Christine Cocker and Trish Hafford-Letchfield, 78–92. Houndsmill: Palgrave Macmillan.

Carr, Sarah. 2014. Critical perspectives on intersectionality. In *Rethinking Anti-Discriminatory and Anti-Oppressive Theories for Social Work Practice*, eds. Christine Cocker and Trish Hafford-Letchfield, 140–153. Houndsmill: Palgrave Macmillan.

Chaney, Paul K. 2011. Mainstreaming intersectional equality for older people? Exploring the impact of quasi-federalism in the UK. *Public Policy and Administration* 28 (1): 21–42.

Costello, Susie, Majorie Quinn, Allison Tatchell, Lynne Jordan and Koula Neophytou. 2015. In the best interests of the child: Preventing female genital cutting. *British Journal of Social Work* 45 (4): 1259–1276.

Crenshaw, K. (1989) Demarginalizing the intersection of race and sex: A black feminist critique of antidiscrimination doctrine, feminist theory and antiracist politics. *University of Chicago Legal Forum* 140: 139–167.

Crenshaw, K. (1991) Mapping the margins: Intersectionality, identity politics, and violence against women of color. *Stanford Law Review* 43 (6): 1241–1299.

Crisp, Beth R. 2017. *The Routledge Handbook of Religion, Spirituality and Social Work*. London: Routledge.

Cuesta, Marta, and Margarets Rämgård. 2016. Intersectionality and elderly care. *International Journal of Qualitative Studies on Health and Well-Being* 11 (1).

Dalrymple, Jane, and Beverley Burke. 2006. *Anti-Oppressive Practice: Social Care and the Law*, 2nd edn. Berkshire: McGraw-Hill Education.

Davis, Ashley, and Sabrina Gentlewarrior. 2015. White privilege and clinical social work practice: Reflections and recommendations. *Journal of Progressive Human Services* 26 (3): 191–206.

Department for Education. 2012. National action plan to tackle child abuse linked to faith or belief. Available at: https://assets.publishing.service.gov.uk › file › Act. Accessed 18 May 2018.

Dinham, Adam. 2018. Religion and belief in health and social care: The case for religious literacy. *International Journal of Human Rights in Healthcare* 11 (2): 83–90.

Dominelli, Lena. 1988. *Anti-Racist Social Work*. London: Macmillan.

Dominelli, Lena, and Eileen McLeod. 1989. Creating a feminist statutory social work. In *Feminist Social Work: Critical Texts in Social Work and the Welfare State*, eds. Lena Dominelli and Eileen McLeod, 101–130. Hampshire: Macmillan.

Duffy, Francis. 2017. A social work perspective on how ageist language, discourses and understandings negatively frame older people and why taking a critical social work stance is essential. *British Journal of Social Work* 47 (7): 2068–2085.

Emejulu, Akmula, and Liza Mügge. 2018. Who is seen and heard in politics? Intersectionality and political representation. *Migration and Citizenship* 6 (1): 44–51.

Fernando, Suman. 2003. *Cultural Diversity, Mental Health and Psychiatry: The Struggle Against Racism*. Hove: Brunner Routledge.

Fernando, Suman, and Frank Keating. 2009. *Mental Health in a Multi-Ethnic Society*, 2nd edn. London: Routledge.

Firmin, Carlene. 2018. Contextualizing case reviews: A methodology for developing systemic safeguarding practices. *Child & Family Social Work* 23: 45–52.

Foner, Nancy, Jan Willem Duyvendak, and Philip Kasinitz. 2019. Super-diversity in everyday life. *Ethnic and Racial Studies* 42 (1): 1–16.

Fong, Rowena. 2004. *Culturally Component Practice with Immigrant and Refugee Children and Families.* New York: Guildford Press.

Furness, Sheila, and Philip A. Gilligan. 2014. 'It never came up': Encouragements and discouragements to addressing religion and belief in professional practice—what do social work students have to say? *The British Journal of Social Work* 44 (3): 763–781.

Garland, Jon, Spalek, Basia and Chakraborti, Neil. 2006. Issues in researching 'hidden' minority ethnic communities. *The British Journal of Criminology* 46 (3): 423–437.

Geldof, Dirk. 2016. Superdiversity and the city. In *Social Work and the City*, ed. Charlotte Williams, 127–149. Houndsmill: Palgrave Macmillan.

Gunn, Alana J., Tina K. Sacks, and Alexis Jemal. 2018. 'That's not me anymore': Resistance strategies for managing intersectional stigmas for women with substance use and incarceration histories. *Qualitative Social Work* 17 (4): 490–508.

Gupta, Anna. 2016. Forced marriage as a safeguarding issue. In *Safeguarding Black Children: Good Practice in Child Protection*, eds. Claudia Bernard and Perlita Harris, 200–215. London: Jessica Kingsley.

Hafford-Letchfield, Trish. 2013. Social work, class and later life. In *Social Class in Later Life: Power, Identity and Lifestyle*, eds. Marvin Formosa and Paul Higgs. Bristol: Policy Press.

Hicks, Stephen. 2014. Social work and gender: An argument for practical accounts. *Qualitative Social Work* 14 (4): 471–487.

Hill Collins, Patricia. 1990. *Black Feminist Thought.* London: Unwin Hyman.

Hill Collins, Patricia. 2015. Intersectionality's definitional dilemmas. *Annual Review of Sociology* 41: 1–20.

Hill Collins, Patricia, and Sirma Bilge. 2016. *Intersectionality.* Cambridge: Polity Press.

Hodge, David R. 2017. Spiritual competence: The key to effective practice with people from diverse backgrounds. In *The Routledge*

Handbook of Religion, Spirituality and Social Work, ed. Beth R. Crisp, 282–290. London: Routledge.

hooks, bell. 1988. *Talking Back: Thinking Feminist, Thinking Black.* Boston, MA: South End Press.

Holloway, Margaret, and Bernard Moss. 2010. *Spirituality and Social Work.* Houndmills: Palgrave Macmillan.

Humphries, Beth. 2008. *Social Work Research for Social Justice.* Basingstoke: Palgrave Macmillan.

Jordan-Zachery, Julia S. 2007. Am I a black woman or a woman who is black? A few thoughts on the meaning of intersectionality. *Politics and Gender* 3 (2): 254–263.

Kantola, Johanna, and Kevät Nousiainen. 2009. Institutionalizing intersectionality in Europe: Introducing the theme. *International Feminist Journal of Politics* 11 (4): 459–477.

Kanyeredzi, Ava. 2018. *Race, Culture, and Gender: Black Female Experiences of Violence and Abuse.* Basingstoke: Palgrave Macmillan.

Keating, Frank. 2016. Racialised communities, producing madness and dangerousness. *Intersectionalities* 5 (3): 173–185.

Keating, Frank. 2015. Linking 'race', mental health and a social model of disability: What are the possibilities? In *Madness, Distress and the Politics of Disablement*, eds. Helen Spandler, Jill Anderson, and Bob Sapey, 127–138. Bristol: Policy Press.

King, Deborah K. 1988. Multiple jeopardy, multiple consciousness: The context of a black feminist ideology. *Signs* 14 (1): 42–72.

King, Andrew, Kathryn Almack, and Rebecca L. Jones. 2019. *Intersections of Ageing, Gender, Sexualities: Multidisciplinary International Perspectives.* Bristol: Policy Press.

Krumer-Nevo, Michal, and Michal Komem. 2015. Intersectionality and critical social work with girls: Theory and practice. *British Journal of Social Work* 45 (4): 1190–1206.

Lavalette, Michael, and Laura Penketh. 2014. *Race, Racism and Social Work: Contemporary Issues and Debates.* Bristol: Policy Press.

Lewis, Gail. 2013. Unsafe travel: Experiencing intersectionality and feminist displacements. *Signs* 38 (4): 869–892.

Mattsson, Tina. 2014. Intersectionality as a useful tool: Anti-oppressive social work and critical reflection. *Affilia* 29 (1): 8–17.

McCall, Leslie. 2005. The complexity of intersectionality. *Signs* 30: 1771–1800.

Mehrotra, Gita. 2010. Toward a continuum of intersectionality theorizing for feminist social work scholarship. *Affilia* 25 (4): 417–430.

Mirza, Heidi S. 2015. Decolonizing higher education: Black feminism and the intersectionality of race and gender. *Journal of Feminist Scholarship* 7/8: 1–12.

Murphy, Yvette, Valerie Hunt, Anna M. Zajicek, Adele N. Norris, and Leah Hamilton. 2009. *Incorporating Intersectionality in Social Work Practice, Research, Policy and Education*. Washington DC: NASW.

Nayak, Suryia, and Rachel Robbins. 2018. *Intersectionality in Social Work: Activism and Practice in Context*. London: Routledge.

Okitikpi, Toyin and Cathy Aymer. 2010. *Key Concepts in Anti-Discriminatory Social Work*. London: Sage.

Pearce, Jenny. 2014. What's going on to safeguard children and young people from child sexual exploitation: A review of local safeguarding children boards' work to protect children from sexual exploitation. *Child Abuse Review* 23(3): 159–170.

Pentaris, Panagiotis. 2012. Religious competence in social work practice: The UK picture. *Social Work and Society* 10 (2): 1–12.

Pitts, John. 2013. Drifting into trouble: Sexual exploitation and gang affiliation. In *Critical Perspectives on Child Sexual Exploitation and Related Trafficking*, eds. M. Melrose and J. Pearce, 23–37. Basingstoke: Palgrave Macmillan.

Prins, Baukje. 2006. Narrative accounts of origins: A blind spot in the intersectional approach? *European Journal of Women's Studies* 13 (3): 277–90.

Rajan-Rankin, Sweta. 2018. Race, embodiment and later life: Re-animating aging bodies of color. *Journal of Aging Studies* 45: 32–38.

Robinson, Mark, Frank Keating, and Steve Robertson. 2011. Ethnicity, gender and mental health. *Diversity in Health and Care* 8 (2): 81–92.

Rodgers, Selena T. 2017. Womanism and Afrocentricity: Understanding the intersection. *Journal of Human Behaviour in the Social Environment* 27 (1–2): 36–47.

Stobart, Eleanor. 2006. Child abuse linked to accusations of 'possession' and 'witchcraft'. London: DfES.

Tedam, Prospera. 2016. Safeguarding children linked to witchcraft. In *Safeguarding Black Children: Good Practice in Child Protection*, eds. Claudia Bernard and Perlita Harris, 216–239. London: Jessica Kingsley.

Tedam, Prospera, and Awura Adjoa. 2017. *The W Word: Witchcraft Labelling and Child Safeguarding in Social Work Practice*. St Albans: Critical Publishing.

Torres, Sandra. 2019. *Ethnicity and Old Age: Expanding Our Imaginations.* Bristol: Policy Press.

Turner, Sandra G., and Tina M. Maschi. 2015. Feminist and empowerment theory and social work practice. *Journal of Social Work Practice* 29 (2): 151–162.

Van Robaeys, Bea, van Ewijk, Hans, and Dierckx, Danielle. 2018. The challenge of superdiversity for the identity of the social work profession: Experiences of social workers in 'De Sloep' in Ghent, Belgium. *International Social Work* 61 (2): 274–288.

Wendt, Sarah, and Nicole Moulding. 2017. The current state of feminism and social work. *Australian Social Work* 70 (3): 261–262.

Westwood, Joanne, 2016. Safeguarding unaccompanied asylum-seeking children. In *Safeguarding Black Children: Good Practice in Child Protection*, eds. Claudia Bernard and Perlita Harris, 239–252. London: Jessica Kingsley.

Wilkens, Jill. 2019. Intersections of aging, gender, class and sexual identity. In *Intersections of Ageing, Gender, Sexualities: Multidisciplinary International Perspectives*, eds. Andrew King, Kathryn Almack, and Rebecca L. Jones, Bristol: Policy Press.

Williams, Charlotte. 1999. Connecting anti-racist and anti-oppressive theory and practice: Retrenchment or reappraisal? *British Journal of Social Work* 29 (2): 211–230.

Williams, Charlotte, and Mark Johnson. 2010. *Race and Ethnicity in the Welfare State*. Maidenhead: Open University Press.

Williams, Charlotte, and Maša Mikola. 2018. From multiculturalism to superdiversity? Narratives of health and wellbeing in an urban neighbourhood. *Social Work & Policy Studies: Social Justice, Practice and Theory* 1(1): 1–24.

Windsong, Elena A. 2018. Incorporating intersectionality into research design: An example using qualitative interviews. *International Journal of Social Research Methodology* 21 (2): 135–147.

Yuval-Davis, Nira. 2006a. Intersectionality and feminist politics. *European Journal of Women's Studies* 13 (3): 193–209.

Yuval-Davis, Nira. 2006b. Belonging and the politics of belonging. *Patterns of Prejudice* 40 (3): 197–214.

2 Intersectionality theory

What is intersectionality?

Intersectionality is generally defined as an interpretive framework for examining the relationship between multiple interlocking systems of oppression that impact gendered experiences (Crenshaw 1989; Hill Collins 1990). Essentially, an intersectionality perspective offers a theoretical tool for understanding how social categories such as race, ethnicity, gender, class, sexual orientation, age, and disability, for example, combine for marginalised groups (Alexander-Floyd 2012; Anthias 2001; Brah and Pheonix 2004; hooks 1994; King 1988; Lewis 2013; Rodgers 2017; Nayak and Robbins 2018; Prins 2006; Yuval-Davis 2006b). Strongly rooted in black feminist thinking and political activism, intersectionality largely emerged when black feminism began to challenge dominant feminist scholarship which privileged gender as a single analytic category, with scant attention paid to race as a category of analysis, resulting in black women's experiences being overlooked or rendered invisible (Hill Collins 1986; Mehrotra 2010). Critical race scholar Kimberlé Crenshaw is credited with coining the term intersectionality in her influential article, 'Demarginalizing the intersection of race and sex: A black feminist critique of anti-discrimination doctrine, feminist theory and antiracist politics', which interrogates the combined effects of race and gender discrimination to conceptualise how systems of oppression affect the lives of black women (Crenshaw 1989). As Crenshaw (1989, 1991) attests, intersectionality centres the relational complexities of how overlapping social identities converge for black women. In Crenshaw's view, intersectionality is a metaphor for the crossroads that black women's multiply-reinforcing experiences need to be understood by virtue of their marginalised social positioning. According to Crenshaw, because multiple forms of subordination overlap for black women,

DOI: 10.4324/9780429467288-2

an intersectional black feminist approach provides an explanatory framework that helps to make sense of their everyday experiences. Challenging white feminist discourses, Crenshaw's intersectional lens eschews a single-axis examination of gender, because the intersectionality of race and class give rise to very different experiences for black women. Crenshaw's conceptualisation of race and gender discrimination was pioneering for providing new meaning to the multi-layered facets of black women's lived experiences. For Crenshaw, an intersectional perspective thus provides a theoretical grounding for looking at race through the lens of gender and feminism through the lens of critical race theory (Crenshaw 1991).

In *Mapping the Margins: Intersectionality, Identity Politics, and Violence Against Women of Color* (1991), Crenshaw expands on the main tenets of her theory of intersectionality for conceptualising a relational approach. Crenshaw distinguishes between three different dimensions of intersectionality in her examination of racism and patriarchy in the context of gender-based violence: structural intersectionality, political intersectionality, and representation intersectionality. Structural intersectionality depicts how social and economic conditions, and factors such as discriminatory practices in employment, affect the everyday lives of black women and play an essential role in circumscribing their experiences. In contrast, political intersectionality directs attention to the way that black women are positioned within at least two subordinated groups that often pursue differing political agendas, so that they are at the margins of feminist and antiracist movements. The third and key concept, representation intersectionality, speaks to the stigmatising discourses about black women's moral worth; for example, the stereotypical ways in which misogynist popular culture represents black women as hypersexualised, sexually promiscuous, and having loose morals. One of the defining features of Crenshaw's conceptualisation of intersectionality is that it foregrounds the profound importance of analysing intersecting structures of inequalities to understand the racialising of black women's gendered experiences. Indeed, as Crenshaw has described, intersectionality offers much to understand multiple axes of differences that are interacting and reinforcing each other, and therefore the importance of a theoretical framework to make sense of the structural conditions that give rise to the racial and gendered dimensions of the oppression experienced by black women.

Over time, intersectionality has become one of the most influential feminist theories and has been used widely as an organising and political tool by feminist and race scholars in different academic disciplines, as well as by activists in social justice movements, to identify and interrogate axes of social inequalities for marginalised groups with intersectional identities (Bilge 2013; Emejulu and Mügge 2018; Hill Collins 2015; Hill Collins and Bilge 2016; Jordan-Zachery 2007; Kantola and Nousiainen 2009; McCall 2005; Mehrotra 2010). In a similar vein, Hill Collins (1990), hooks (1989), and Lorde (1984), seek to conceptualise black women's experiences within an intersectional framework to offer insights into how the interacting structural dimensions of race, class, and gender inequalities affect them. Thus, all three scholars stress the interlocking matrix of multiple and intersecting oppressions as a central feature of intersectionality.

According to this viewpoint, an intersectional frame of analysis is better able to elucidate insights into how black women will experience gender discrimination differently to white women and will also experience racial discrimination differently to black men as a result of their racialised gendered location (Crenshaw 1991; Hill Collins 1990; Lorde 1984).

Importantly, intersectional feminist scholarship focuses on the ways in which the critical tools offered by intersectionality can probe layers of oppression. In particular, from an intersectional perspective, there is the potential to disrupt the privileging of gender over race and race over gender, because attention is drawn to the centrality of the intersection of multiple forms of oppression that simultaneously accentuate black women's lived realities. As intersectional feminist scholars have pointed out, a critical set of tools is necessary for analysing overlapping and intersecting forms of oppression (Mirza 2014; Prins 2006; Yuval-Davis 2006b). Recognising this need eschews the hierarchies of oppression trope for a more nuanced understanding of the interacting systemic processes of race, gender, social class, and other dimensions of social identity.

Definitional issues with intersectionality

For the most part, feminist scholars are clear that intersectionality offers various possibilities for its theoretical and methodological tools to be used in the study of inequalities. At the same time, however, exactly what constitutes intersectionality is contested by a number of feminist scholars (e.g., Hill Collins 2015; Hulko 2009; May 2015; MacKinnon 2013; McCall 2005; Mirza 2016; Nash 2017). Indeed, Nash (2017) refers to the 'intersectional wars' when she makes the point that feminist debates about intersectionality have become very contentious.

As Hulko makes clear, different terminology has been used to describe intersectionality, including *paradigm, framework, theory, lens,* and *perspective* (Hulko 2009, 44). At a more general level, scholars such as Lewis (2013), MacKinnon (2013), and McCall (2005) have criticised its complexity, open-ended nature, and theoretical vagueness, as well as methodological issues of studying it. Some scholars argue that intersectionality is often misapplied and misunderstood or dismissed as too abstract (Hill Collins 2015; May 2015; MacKinnon 2013; McCall 2005), and others question whether intersectionality is a theory or a conceptual framework (Choo and Ferree 2010). Furthermore, despite recognising the critical powers of intersectionality, black feminist scholar Hill Collins notes that it has a number of definitional problems and crucially characterises intersectionality in three different ways: (1) as a field of study, (2) as an analytical strategy that provides new angles of vision, and (3) as critical praxis to examine social justice projects (Hill Collins 2015, 1). Similarly, Mirza calls into question the universal usage of intersectionality and contends that 'intersectionality has become a buzzword for white feminists: a political concept devoid of any real meaning' (Mirza 2016, 1).

Moreover, as May acknowledges, we cannot ignore that the theory has been moved away from its strong foundations in critical race thinking and inclusive social justice orientation; arguing its potential for transformation and change, May's contention is that intersectionality is applied too widely now, and sometimes in superficial ways, so its radical history and transformative vision are being diluted. As May explains, feminist scholars in a range of disciplines have used intersectionality extensively as an analytical frame for diverse sets of practices, and an unintended consequence is that in making the concept 'more "universal" via deracialization and depoliticization … such that its deep focus on critical race theorising' is ignored (May 2015, 18). May reflects on what she refers to as the co-optation of intersectionality, that is, the appropriation of the theory by white feminists, whereby it has become more of a buzzword in some feminist writings (May 2014).

Similarly, critiques have been made by a range of black feminist and critical race scholars such as Bilge (2013), hooks (1984), Joseph (2015), Mirza (2016), and Nash (2017) suggesting that the discourse of intersectionality has been universalised; as Bilge (2013) has observed, some feminist scholars use intersectionality as a substitute for gender without even marginally touching on race.

What these different debates illuminate is intersectionality's significance as an explanatory framework, in spite of the different standpoint approaches. For some, the focus is on social categories of identities, whilst others see intersectionality as to do with mutually reinforcing systems of oppression; what is clear is that there is broad agreement that intersectional approaches allow us to dig deeper into the structural forces at play in reproducing inequality.

Intersectional approaches in social work

What, then, is the place of intersectionality in social work? Intersectionality is a growing area of study in social work literature that now warrants an entry in the *Encyclopaedia of Social Work* (Yamada et al. 2016). Intersectionality has enjoyed broad application in social work for understanding individual, organisational, and societal inequalities and their impact on service users' lived experiences.

Intersectionality has also been particularly used to theorise social work across a diverse array of topics, such as social work education and pedagogical approaches (Beltran and Mehrotra 2015; Bryson and Bennet-Anyikwa 2003; Bubar et al. 2016; Chi-Pun Liu 2017 Jani et al. 2011; Joseph 2015; Murphy et al. 2009; Robinson et al. 2016; Yamada et al. 2015); praxis and activism (Nayak and Robbins 2018); domestic violence (Ramon 2015); mental health (Carr 2014; Keating 2016; Walton and Oyewuwo-Gassikia 2017); children and families (Krumer-Nevo and Komem 2015); feminist social work (Eyal-Lubling and Krumer-Nevo 2016; Mattsson 2014; Mehrotra 2010); social work research (Zufferey 2015; Hulko 2015) and diversity in social work (Van Impe and Arteel 2018).

According to Mattsson, intersectionality as an organising frame can be used in reflective practice and critical reflection for understanding the complexity of categories of identities and power relationships in social work education and practice. In her seminal article on intersectionality as a useful tool for social work, Mattsson (2014) employs McCall's (2005) three approaches to the study of intersectionality, namely intercategorical, intracategorical, and anticategorical to explore how they might be used to aid critical reflection in social work. McCall defines an intercategorical approach as being concerned with understanding how identity is shaped by social determinants, and how groups from different social backgrounds are affected by structural inequalities and their social circumstances. The second approach, which she calls intracategorical, focuses on heterogeneity within groups and in particular the experiences of those situated within multiple intersecting identities. The third, an anticategorical approach, concerns ideas and interpretation and contests the notion of fixed social categories such as gender, sex, and race, by positing fluidity in these categories which are largely determined by social structures. Thus, as Mattsson observes, intersectionality enables alternative ways of understanding how social inequalities shape service users' multi-layered experiences, and most importantly, their encounters with welfare services. According to both Mattsson (2014) and Mehrota (2010), McCall's ideas about intersectionality offer routes for different approaches to critical reflection for social work, as intersectionality provides a broader framework to understand the social and contextual lives of service users.

In particular, feminist social work scholars attest that as praxis—i.e. reflection and action—is a core tenet of intersectionality, it lends itself to bridging the gap between theory and practice. As Nayak and Robbins (2018) indicate, an intersectional lens can help social workers engage with the shared values underpinning social work traditions and may address power and inequalities in social work for advancing a social justice approach. More specifically, intersectional theory is used as the lens for understanding the processes of structural and institutional discrimination impacting the lives of service users (Murphy et al. 2009). While it could be argued that intersectionality is born out of emancipatory collective action that can be at odds with the individual case-managed approach of UK statutory social work, it could also be argued that as a theoretical tool, intersectionality can help sharpen the analysis that is needed for advancing the human rights and social justice principles that are central to social work (IFSW 2014). In contrast, other scholars have highlighted that intersectionality can inform social work practice and community organising and activism around a range of topics, including Islamophobia, immigration, violence against women and girls, and citizenship policy (Nayak and Robbins 2018). Furthermore, intersectionality can help with developing analyses of the institutional cultures and organisational structures of social services delivery. It is precisely because of its potential for transformative change that an intersectional lens can offer rich insights into the contextual nature of lived experiences.

It is certainly the case that social workers will repeatedly be brought face-to-face with the adverse consequences of structural inequalities and the issues confronting people with marginalised identities and statuses. As the International Social Work Federation declaration makes clear, social workers are working every day with life at its extremes, witnessing the highs and lows of human capabilities and behaviour (IFSW 2014, 3). In this sense, it is crucial for social workers to understand the different dimensions of inequalities and forms of oppression for promoting diversity, equality, and social justice in social work. Therefore, having the tools for critical engagement with the interconnecting systems of oppression (e.g., disablism, racism, sexism, heterosexism), alongside an acute awareness of your own positionality, is key for developing approaches to practice that are grounded in anti-oppressive principles. More specifically, when working with vulnerable and disadvantaged individuals and groups, a social justice perspective that can interrogate the role of the state, and the organisational structures of social work in particular, is of crucial importance for good social work practice that does not reproduce oppression. There is thus a clear case to be made that intersectionality as an organising framework can equip social workers with the tools of analysis that are essential for navigating the constraints and challenges for marginalised groups affected by multiple intersecting identities. Moreover, the employment of an intersectional approach offers social workers tools to develop the capacity to work with the interactional dynamics and ethical complexities that arise when intervening with a diverse range of individuals and groups in our multicultural and multifaith society (Bernard 2019a; Bernard 2019b).

Conclusion

In this chapter, I have given an overview of some of the theoretical discussions surrounding intersectionality, an organising concept to analyse and interrogate categories of social identities such as gender, race, age, sexual orientation, disability, and class, as well as systems of oppression. In particular, feminist scholars have recognised intersectionality as an important critical approach for attending to systemic inequalities and relations of power. I have also considered the different ways in which intersectional approaches have been construed in social work scholarship and research to open up new ways for understanding the lived experiences of users of social services. Intersectionality certainly offers tools for expanding social workers' understandings of how mutually reinforcing oppressions are experienced by diverse individuals and groups in their environmental and social context. What I find most striking about an intersectional perspective is that it offers us a conceptual framework that can facilitate a better understanding of how interlocking oppressions manifest in everyday experiences. To this end, since social work can be seen as playing a mediating role between the individual and society (Parton 1996) and has a key part to play in remedying issues of social inequalities (Mattsson 2014), the analytical contribution of intersectionality is therefore beneficial, as it aligns very well with the profession's value base and aspirations for utilising empowerment models for advancing transformative change.

Reflective questions

- In terms of self-reflection, how might an intersectional framework help you to understand your own positionality and social location?
- How might intersectionality be used as an analytical tool to make sense of the person in environment?
- What do you understand by the term interlocking oppression?
- Can you think of any examples of ways in which intersectionality can be used to develop awareness of structural inequalities and power relations in social work practice?
- To what extent do you think intersectionality can help with developing reflective practice?
- In what ways can intersectionality help with furthering social justice goals in social work?

References

Alexander-Floyd, Nikol G. 2012. Disappearing acts: Reclaiming intersectionality in the social sciences in a post-black feminist era. *Feminist Formations* 24 (1): 1–25.

Anthias, Floya. 2001. The material and the symbolic in theorizing social stratification. *British Journal of Sociology* 52 (3): 367–90.

Beltran, Ramona, and Gita Mehrotra. 2015. Honoring our intellectual ancestors: A feminist of color treaty for creating allied collaboration. *Affilia* 30 (1): 106–116.

Bernard, Claudia. 2019a. Working with cultural and religious diversity. In *The Child's World*, 3rd edn., eds. Jan Horwath and Dendy Platt, 659–665. London: Jessica Kingsley.

Bernard, Claudia. 2019b. Using an intersectional lens to examine the child sexual exploitation of black adolescents. In *Child Sexual Exploitation: Theory to Practice*, ed., Jenny Pearce, 193–208. Bristol: Policy Press.

Bilge, Sirma. 2013. Intersectionality undone: Saving intersectionality from feminist intersectionality studies. *Du Bois Review* 10 (2): 405–424.

Brah, Avtar, and Ann Phoenix. 2004. Ain't I a woman? Revisiting intersectionality. *Journal of International Women's Studies* 5 (3): 75–86.

Bryson, B. J., and Victoria Bennet-Anyikwa. 2003. The teaching and learning experience: Deconstructing and creating space using a feminist pedagogy. *Race, Gender and Class* 10 (2): 131–146.

Bubar, Roe, Karina Cespedes, and Kimberly Bundy-Fazioli. 2016. Intersectionality and social work: Omissions of race, class, and sexuality in graduate school education. *Journal of Social Work Education* 52 (3): 283–296.

Carr, Sarah. 2014. Critical perspectives on intersectionality. In *Rethinking Anti-Discriminatory and Anti-Oppressive Theories for Social Work Practice*, eds. Christine Cocker and Trish Hafford-Letchfield, 140–153. Basingstoke: Palgrave Macmillan.

Cho, Sumi, Kimberlé Crenshaw, and Leslie McCall. 2013. Toward a field of intersectionality studies: Theory, applications, and praxis. *Signs* 38 (4): 785–810.

Choo, Hae Yeon and Myra Marx Ferree. 2010. Practicing intersectionality in sociological research: A critical analysis of inclusions, interactions, and institutions in the study inequalities. *Sociological Theory* 28 (2): 129–149.

Chi-Pun Liu, Ben. 2017. Intersectional impact of multiple identities of social work education in the UK. *Journal of Social Work* 17 (2): 226–242.

Crenshaw, Kimberlé. 1989. Demarginalizing the intersection of race and sex: A black feminist critique of anti-discrimination doctrine, feminist theory and antiracist politics. *University of Chicago Legal Forum* 140: 139–167.

Crenshaw, Kimberlé. 1991. Mapping the margins: Intersectionality, identity politics, and violence against women of color. *Stanford Law Review* 43 (6): 1241–1299.

Emejulu, Akmula, and Liza Mügge. 2018. Who is seen and heard in politics? Intersectionality and political representation. *Migration and Citizenship* 6 (1): 44–51.

Eyal-Lubling, Roni, and Michal Krumer-Nevo. 2016. Feminist social work: Practice and theory of practice. *Social Work* 61 (3): 245–254.

Hill Collins, Patricia. 1986. Learning from the outsider within: The sociological significance of black feminist thought. *Social Problems* 33 (6): 514–532.

Hill Collins, Patricia. 1990. *Black Feminist Thought.* London: Unwin Hyman.

Hill Collins, Patricia. 2015. Intersectionality's definitional dilemmas. *Annual Review of Sociology* 41: 1–20.

Hill Collins, Patricia, and Sirma Bilge. 2016. *Intersectionality.* Cambridge: Polity Press.

hooks, bell. 1988. *Talking Back: Thinking Feminist, Thinking Black.* Boston, MA: South End Press.

hooks, bell. 1994. *Teaching to Transgress: Education as the Practice of Freedom.* New York: Routledge.

Hulko, Wendy. 2009. The time-and context-contingent nature of intersectionality and interlocking oppressions. *Affilia* 24 (1): 44–55.

Hulko, Wendy. 2015. Operationalizing intersectionality in feminist social work research: Reflections and techniques from research with equity-seeking groups. In *Feminisms in Social Work Research: Promise and Possibilities for Justice-Based Knowledge,* eds. Stéphanie Wahab, Ben Anderson-Nathe, Christina Gringeri, 68–89. Abingdon: Routledge.

IFSW (International Federation of Social Workers). 2014. Global agenda for social work and social development: First report— promoting social and economic equalities. *International Social Work,* 57 (4): 3–16.

Jani, Jayshree S., Dean Pierce, Larry Ortiz, and Lynda Sowbel. 2011. Access to intersectionality, content to competence: Deconstructing social work education diversity standards. *Journal of Social Work Education* 47 (2): 283–301.

Jibrin, Sarah Mamdouh Ibrahim, and Rekia Jibrin. 2015. Revisiting intersectionality: Reflections on theory and praxis. *Trans-Scripts* 5: 7–24.

Jordan-Zachery, Julia S. 2007. Am I a black woman or a woman who is black? A few thoughts on the meaning of intersectionality. *Politics and Gender* 3 (2): 254–263.

Joseph, Ameil. 2015. Beyond intersectionalities of identity or interlocking analyses of difference: Confluence and the problematic of 'anti'-oppression. *Intersectionalities* 4 (1): 15–39.

Kantola, Johanna and Kevät Nousiainen. 2009. Institutionalizing intersectionality in Europe: Introducing the theme. *International Feminist Journal of Politics* 11 (4): 459–477.

Keating, Frank. 2016. Racialised communities, producing madness and dangerousness. *Intersectionalities* 5 (3): 173–185.

King, Deborah K. 1988. Multiple jeopardy, multiple consciousness: The context of a black feminist ideology. *Signs* 14 (1): 42–72.

Krumer-Nevo, Michal, and Michal Komem. 2015. Intersectionality and critical social work with girls: Theory and practice. *British Journal of Social Work* 45 (4): 1190–1206.

Lewis, Gail. 2013. Unsafe travel: Experiencing intersectionality and feminist dis- placements. *Signs* 38 (4): 869–92.

Lorde, Audre. 1984. *Sister Outsider.* Berkeley, California: Crossing Press.

MacKinnon, Catharine A. 2013. Intersectionality as method: A note. *Signs* 38 (41): 1019–1030.

Mattsson, Tina. 2014. Intersectionality as a useful tool. *Affilia* 29 (1): 8–17.

May, Vivian M. 2014. 'Speaking to the void'? Intersectionality critiques and epistemic backlash. *Hypatia* 29 (1): 94–112.

May, Vivian M. 2015. *Pursuing Intersectionality, Unsettling Dominant Imaginaries.* New York: Routledge.

McCall, Leslie. 2005. The complexity of intersectionality studies: Theory, application, praxis. *Signs* 30 (3): 1771–1800.

Mehrotra, Gita. 2010. Toward a continuum of intersectionality theorizing for feminist social work. *Affilia* 25 (4): 417–430.

Mirza, Heidi S. 2014. Decolonizing higher education: Black feminism and the intersectionality of race and gender. *Journal of Feminist Scholarship* 7/8: 1–12.

Mirza, Heidi S. 2016. Black feminist futures: White feminist pasts. *Skin Deep*. Available at: www.skindeepmag.com/online-articles/black-feminist-futures-white-feminist-pasts. Accessed 4 January 2019.

Murphy, Yvette, Valerie Hunt, Anna M. Zajicek, Adele N. Norris, and Leah Hamilton. 2009. *Incorporating Intersectionality in Social Work Practice, Research, Policy and Education*. Washington, DC: NASW.

Nash, Jennifer C. 2008. Re-thinking intersectionality. *Feminist Review* 89 (1): 1–15.

Nash, Jennifer C. 2017. Intersectionality and its discontents. *American Quarterly* 69 (1): 117–129.

Nayak, Suryia, and Rachel Robbins. 2018. *Intersectionality in Social Work: Activism and Practice in Context*. London: Routledge

Parton, Nigel. 1996. An introduction. In *Social Theory, Social Change and Social Work*, ed. Nigel Parton, 4–18. Abingdon: Routledge.

Prins, Baukje. 2006. Narrative accounts of origins: A blind spot in the intersectional approach? *European Journal of Women's Studies* 13 (3): 277–290.

Ramon, Shula. 2015. Intersectionalities: Intimate partner domestic violence and mental health within the European context. *Intersectionalities*, 4 (2): 76–100.

Robinson, Michael A., Bronwyn Cross-Denny, Karen Kyeunghae Lee, Lisa Marie Werkmeister Rozas, and Ann-Marie Yamada. 2016. Teaching note—Teaching intersectionality: Transforming cultural competence content in social work education. *Journal of Social Work Education* 52 (4): 509–517.

Rodgers, Selena T. 2017. Womanism and Afrocentricity: Understanding the intersection. *Journal of Human Behaviour in the Social Environment* 27 (1–2): 36–47.

Van Impe, Anja, and Inge Arteel. 2018. Intersectionality in social work: A correction of the hype about super diversity. *Tijdschrift voor Genderstudies*, 21 (1): 75–79.

Walton, Quenette L., and Olubunmi Basirat Oyewuwo-Gassikia. 2017. The case for black girl magic: Application of a strengths based intersectional framework to working with black women with depression. *Affilia* 32 (4): 461–475.

Wendt, Sarah, and Nicole Moulding. 2016. *Contemporary Feminisms in Social Work Practice.* London: Routledge.

Yamada, Ann-Marie, Lisa Marie Werkmeister Rozas, and Bronwyn Cross-Denny. 2015. Intersectionality and social work. In *Encyclopaedia of Social Work Online*, 21st edn. New York, NY: NASW Press and Oxford University Press.

Yuval-Davis, Nira. 2006. Belonging and the politics of belonging. *Patterns of Prejudice* 40 (3): 197–214.

Zufferey, Carole. 2015. Intersectional feminism and social work responses to homelessness. In *Feminisms in Social Work Research: Promise and Possibilities for Justice-Based Knowledge*, eds. Stéphanie Wahab, Ben Anderson-Nathe, and Christina Gringeri, 90–102. Abingdon: Routledge.

3 Employing intersectionality in children and families social work

This chapter explores the ways in which intersectionality can be applied in children and families social work. In particular, it will focus on interventions with children in the child protection system, to show how an intersectional approach can be used to make sense of risk and protective factors for children in danger of harm. The aim here is to show how intersectionality, as a theoretical model, can be used as an organising framework in assessments of children's development needs, as well as for parenting capacity and family and environmental factors when there are safeguarding concerns. I begin with a brief overview of some of the multiple forms of abuse and psychosocial harms that children experience to illuminate the key issues that social workers in children and families social work will encounter, and then discuss how intersectionality can be employed as an organising framework in assessments.

Social work with children and families

It is no surprise that abuse and neglect are the most common causes of children coming to the attention of children's social care (HM Government 2018). Understandably, as the demographic composition of children in the UK has become more ethnically diverse, there is a much broader range of safeguarding issues that social workers have to respond to. Indeed, attention should especially be drawn to the notion that there are emergent forms of abuse and harmful behaviours that raise questions concerning belief systems and norms about parenting and child-rearing practices, challenging understandings of thresholds of need, and for making judgements about harm (Bernard 2019; Bernard and Gupta 2008; Bernard and Harris 2019). For example, there may be abuse linked

DOI: 10.4324/9780429467288-3

to faith and cultural beliefs, such as accusations of witchcraft or spirit possession (Briggs and Whittaker 2018; DfE 2012; Tedam 2016; Tedam and Adjoa 2017), female genital mutilation (Connelly et al. 2018); honour-based violence and forced marriage (Alijah and Chantler 2015; Costello et al. 2015; Gupta 2016).

Additionally, there is a burgeoning literature capturing the experiences of children living in families with multiple adversities such as poverty, deprivation, homelessness, parental mental health, and substance misuse problems, as well as those exposed to situations of risk through domestic violence (Morris et al. 2018; Featherstone et al. 2014; Featherstone et al. 2018; Keddell and Hyslop 2019). In recent years, there is also recognition that children who are gang-associated or living in gang-affected neighbourhoods have increased exposure to multiple stressors, such as county lines, involving children transporting drugs from cities to rural areas, as well as children going missing from home and care, and at risk of sexual exploitation (Beckett et al. 2013; Firmin 2018; Firmin et al. 2016). Moreover, there is broad agreement among researchers that racial disproportionality and disparity in child welfare means that black children are over-represented in the child welfare system (Owen and Statham 2009; Selwyn et al. 2010; Tilbury and Thoburn 2009). Key literature also highlights that children with disabilities are at greater risk of abuse and harm (McDonnell et al. 2018; Shannon and Tappan 2011; Stalker and McArthur 2012).

In child welfare debates, there has been increased attention given to the needs and experiences of unaccompanied asylum-seeking and refugee children who are separated from their parents, to better understand their increase risks of being trafficked and exploited (Clayton et al. 2019; Ehntholt et al. 2018; Ni Raghallaigh 2014; Westwood 2016), as well as widespread recognition of the issues concerning children who are trafficked to the UK for domestic slavery and exploitation and who are especially vulnerable to multiple forms of maltreatment (Stobart 2006; Bokhari 2008). In several ways, the literature demonstrates that some children are living in the most trying circumstances because they are in families with uncertain legal status who have no recourse to public funds (Bernard and Harris 2016).

The legal and policy context of child and family social work

In terms of the legal and policy contexts for safeguarding children, the Children Act 1989 provides the statutory basis for social workers' interventions in families. Under the Children Act 1989, children's services departments have particular duties to safeguard and promote the welfare of all children living in their area covering children in need of support, children in need of protection from abuse and neglect, and children looked after by local authorities. Specifically, Section 17 of the Children Act 1989 requires local authorities to provide support to a child in need in their area, whilst under section 47 they are required to carry out investigations if they believe a child has suffered or is at risk of significant harm as a result of abuse and neglect (HM Government 1989). Statutory guidance describing the roles and responsibilities of the key agencies who are required to work together to safeguard and promote the welfare of children is set out in *Working Together to Safeguard Children* (HM Government 2018). Core principles of the Children Act are keeping the child in focus, the welfare of the child is paramount, maintaining the best interest of the child, and working in partnership with families.

The *Framework for the Assessment of Children in Need and Their Families* (Department of Health 2000) sets out the essential information that needs to be gathered to make professional judgements about need. The Assessment Framework comprises three domains: (1) the child's development needs; (2) parenting capacity; and (3) the family and environmental factors framing families' experiences.

The Assessment Framework is deployed as a structure to systematically gather, analyse, understand, and record information about children's and families' circumstances when they come to the attention of children's social services (Department of Health 2000). A crucial aspect of the Assessment Framework is that it provides a useful tool for social workers to undertake more analytic assessments of

Assessment Framework

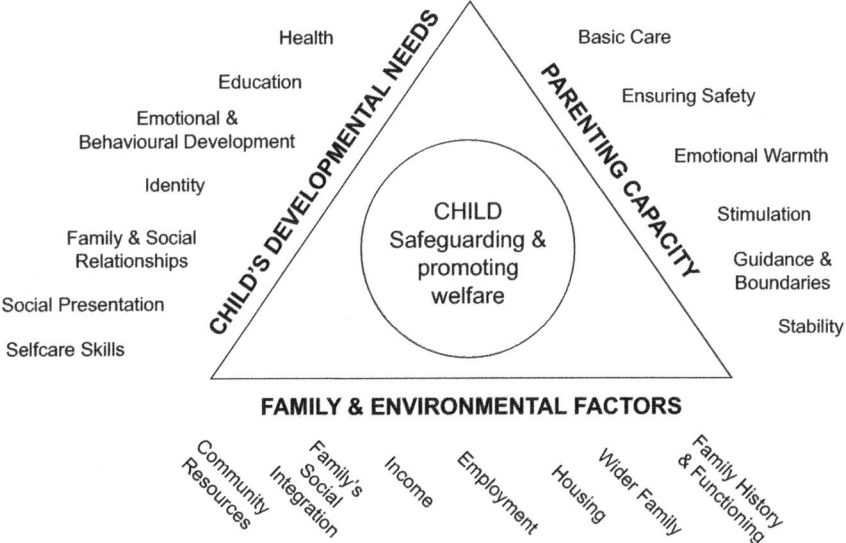

Figure 3.1. The assessment framework

Source: Department of Health (2000)

the issues that are not only affecting children at an intra-familial level, but also the contextual factors that impact the parents' resources and abilities to care for their children. Crucially, the Assessment Framework was developed to determine whether children are in need, as well as to make assessments of significant harm they may be experiencing. I therefore contend that intersectionality aligns well with the Assessment Framework as it offers social workers a frame for assessing the intersectional nature of the factors associated with the three dimensions of the triangle to understand the lived experiences of children and families. Intersectionality thus lends itself to the Assessment Framework as it can provide the critical tools that are needed to make sense of the factors for contextual safeguarding (Firmin 2018) and relationship-based practice (Ruch 2014). In short, the Assessment Framework serves as a tool to assist social workers in making sense of the complex and diverse range of safeguarding concerns which raise critical issues about ways of engaging effectively with families coming from diverse cultural and religious backgrounds.

This whistle-stop tour has given you a glimpse of the multiple forms of abuse and psychosocial harms that children experience. I have also provided a brief overview of the statutory and policy framework for social work interventions to respond to concerns about children's welfare. Against this context, it can be seen that social workers will need to be especially sensitive and attuned to the lived experiences of children and families. Social workers require good knowledge, skills, and expertise to navigate the intricacies and nuances of children's circumstances in order to provide competent intervention to promote their best interests and to safeguard their welfare. In the next section, I will look at the ways in which intersectionality can be employed to assess the needs of children and understand the social context of their experiences.

Case study: Sam

Family composition:

Maggie (28)
Peter (34)
Sam (12)
Charlie (12)
Sarah (8)

Maggie and Peter have three children, namely twins Sam and Charlie, and younger daughter Sarah. Maggie and Peter are married and have been together for 14 years. Maggie is White Irish, and Peter is Black African. Maggie's family did not approve of Maggie and Peter's union and there is no contact with Maggie's family, aside from her younger sister Kerrie, who regularly see Sam, Charlie, and Sarah, and who lived with the family for a while; Peter travels frequently for work, mainly to Africa, where his extended family remain. The family

---

have not had prior contact with Children's Services, although they were supported by the Early Help service in 2014 due to concerns about Charlie's behaviour; he was diagnosed with ADHD in 2015, so the family was supported by universal and health services.

Children's Services became involved with the family when concerns were raised about Sam's health and well-being. Sam's school referred her to Children's Services following an overdose attempt in school, when she took 20 pills of paracetamol; they have raised concerns about Sam struggling with her sense of identity and exploring her sexuality, as she dressed regularly in what school describes as a 'masculine' manner. The school is concerned that the parents were not responding to Sam's needs; Maggie has reported Sam is going through a 'phase', and Peter is not acknowledging that Sam has any mental health problems. The school also reported concerns that Charlie is also rejecting Sam, and that the rejection has been difficult for Sam as the twins were previously very close. The parents express their frustration as Sam has refused to attend church with the rest of the family; they feel that she is being a 'rebellious teenager' and are keen to get support to put her 'back in line'. The school expressed concern that Sam's academic attainment has been impacted by the current situation and are worried that unless Sam and the family receive support, her academic progress will be in jeopardy.

Discussion

As can be seen in this case scenario, the intersection of multiple elements including gender, race, age, religion, and sexuality will need to be considered to make sense of the lived experiences of Sam and her siblings. An intersectional framework offers some analytical tools that can be used in conjunction with the Assessment Triangle to help us understand the developmental needs of a vulnerable child such as Sam. We can see that Sam clearly meets the 'children in need' criteria as set out in section 17 of the Children Act 1989. Most worryingly, it has been indicated that she has some mental health problems and has already attempted suicide. It is not surprising that there are major concerns about Sam's emotional well-being and an assessment of increase suicide risk is therefore crucial to identify immediate or potential risks. Attempted suicide is a traumatic experience not only for Sam but will also have adversely affected her siblings and parents. Getting the right kind of mental health support for Sam will thus be crucial, and her family will also require emotional and practical support to deal with the after-effects. We know from research that black and ethnic minority individuals face unique challenges and that they often have poorer outcomes in the mental health system (Keating 2019). Additionally, research suggests that suicidal children often do not know where or how to access help, and when seen by mental health practitioners often do not feel listened to (Gilmore et al. 2019).

Furthermore, Gilmore et al. (2019) identified that there is a silence around suicidality within the conversations that mental health practitioners have with children. They note that the word suicide is avoided, and the term self-harm is used instead, thus contributing to the silence about suicide. Therefore, engaging an intersectional lens can help us uncover some of the issues to begin to get an understanding of what is taking place for Sam and her family, as Frank Keating (2016) noted when he invoked the significance of an intersectional lens for helping us to understand the contexts for racialised groups in relation to their mental health.

It is important to keep in mind that adolescence is a critical time in Sam's development, as she is likely to be exploring her gendered identity and beginning to develop a sense of her place in the world (McLean et al. 2017). Of course, it will also be crucial for the social worker to consider Sam's self-concept as a mixed-race child. Consider, for instance, that Sam may be feeling unsafe both at school and at home. Thus, the goal here is to gain an understanding of what life is like for Sam in this family setting and how she makes sense of her experiences (Bernard and Thomas 2016). Key tenents of inter-sectionality such as power, oppression, and identity help to deepen our understanding of how Sam as a mixed-race girl is positioned within interlocking systems of oppression, constellated around age, race, gender, social class, and sexuality.

Whilst there is no indication given in the referral of the family's class background, issues of social class are important considerations. For instance, if the family is from a lower socio-economic background, it will be important to recognise that inequality and disadvantage will contribute to the adversities faced by black and minority ethnic children, making the children in this family at greater risk of negative outcomes (Barn and Kirton, 2015; Bernard and Thomas, 2016; Bernard and Harris, 2019; Bywaters et al. 2016). More generally, inter-sectionality provides social workers with some tools to understand the dynamics inherent in Sam's class situation and to identify the systemic barriers associated with class constraints for her family (Strier et al. 2012).

Notably, Sam may be experiencing peer pressure as a result of prevailing norms about femininity and may be more vulnerable to harassment and bullying as a result of her emerging sexual orientation. Childhood gender identity and sexuality issues remain poorly understood and it will be important not to assume that she is only going through a phase. During the development period of adolescence, the transition between childhood and adulthood, there are physical, cognitive, and emotional changes, as well as the need for acceptance (Tatum 2004). That a mental health label has stigmatising effects is an important consideration, and in addressing this particularly relevant issue, an intersectional lens will help to avoid a focus on pathology (Krumer-Nevo et al. 2015).

Given the need to hear Sam's views, it will be crucial not to under-estimate her agency to express her feelings. Tait and Wosu (2019) stress the importance of listening to the voice of the child to understand the relational world of children and the experiences that shape their lives. In short, the social worker should know how to build rapport and create opportunities to develop trust with Sam to enable open discussions about painful experiences and to navigate the obstacles that she faces. To assess Sam's psychological and emotional well-being, the social worker will need to sensitively listen to her in order to create the conditions for her to feel safe enough to articulate how she sees her gender and racial identities and an intersectional lens is beneficial for making sense of these. For example, an intersectional approach helps us to consider, to use Thorne's words, that Sam 'is at the border from "child" to "teen" and is entering the shifting contours of identity and experiences of self' (Thorne 2004, 404). Thus, intersectionality can enable an understanding of the entanglement of several areas of subordination for Sam in her transition from childhood to adolescence.

As religion is an important dimension of family life in this household, it will be important to establish how Sam identifies spiritually or religiously, as her parents may have particular doctrinal expectations of her that may present barriers to her development and expression of her gendered identity.

Specifically, as an organising concept for making sense of multiple identities, an intersectional framework can facilitate the asking of sensitive questions that will help inform assessments of the layered experiences of Sam. Indeed, an intersectional analysis offers the tools that will ensure that the issues relating to Sam's identity are fully interrogated and understood to inform the decision-making about her needs. Ultimately, intersectionality can help us to consider how this coming together of multiple identities may affect Sam's experiences as well as her problematic sense of belonging, which may lead to increased isolation. More precisely, an intersectional analysis helps us to understand the multiple dimensions of Sam's situation to create a care plan that can take account of her intersectional identities, and thus meet her myriad needs.

From the information in this referral, there is a good reason to believe that Sam is in an unsupportive home environment and there may be indications of family-related risk factors for abuse and neglect. In light of the concerns flagged, it will be critical to work alongside the parents to assess parenting capacity and familial and environmental factors that are impacting the parents' capability to provide consistent supportive care. An intersectional lens will enable an exploration of the contextual factors that are impacting this interracial family's day-to-day lived experiences (Tizard and Phoenix 1995). Indeed, intersectional social work scholars such as Mattsson (2014), Mehrotra (2010), and Murphy et al. (2009) have stressed the need to focus on the complexity of issues that are important for understanding experiences shaped by socially constructed divisions. In particular, bearing in mind that Sam is from an interracial family, where religion is an important dimension of family life, an intersectionality frame of reference offers a more critically reflective space to interrogate the various identities and their roles in shaping the cultural values of the family, and perhaps most importantly, how familial relationships are experienced and understood (Atkin and Chol Yoo 2019). These factors will be important as meanings the parents attribute to their religious beliefs might significantly influence their parenting practices concerning guidance and boundaries, and especially parental expectations around gender conformity. For instance, Sam's parents may also find it difficult to have a potentially uncomfortable conversation about sex and Sam's developing sexuality. In these circumstances, it can be very challenging to make effective assessment and intervention when working with disguised compliance or parental resistance. In assessing Maggie's and Peter's parenting capabilities, it will be important to engage both parents to understand something of their family history and functioning as well as their caregiving skills, their relationship together, and how they see the parent-child relationship with regards to Sam. It is notable that Maggie was only 14 years old when she began a relationship with Peter, who was then already 20 years old, and that Maggie was only 16 when she had the twins. Given that parenting for Maggie started at such an early age and with what appears to be a lack of supportive family networks around her, it will be important to understand how she now experiences her parenting role, and intersectionality is therefore a helpful conceptual framework from which to understand her experiences and circumstances. Moreover, as the referral indicates, Peter regularly travels to Africa for his work, so it will be important to understand how these absences affect his day-to-day parenting. It will thus be vital to understand each parent's view and attitudes on gender roles, the distribution of power in the family, and the implications for the arrangement of parenting roles within it. Intersectionality offers the possibility to unpack the gendered power relations for prompting the kind of questions that will elicit Maggie and Peter's perception of their relationship, as well as their mothering and fathering role. More importantly, an intersectional lens enables us to be attentive to gendered biases in social work, where there is a tendency to hold mothers responsible and render fathers invisible when there are problems in the family (Bernard 2013; Davis and Krane 1997). Most notably, an intersectional frame of reference helps to cultivate a deeper appreciation of how mother-blaming discourses pervade social work practice (Bernard and Harris 2019; Featherstone 2010). An intersectional orientation also enables us to have a more nuanced exploration of racialised beliefs and to question stereotypical images about black men (such as absent fathers, feckless, or aggressive) which contributes to how black fathers are thought about and responded to in social work practice (Gupta and Featherstone 2016; Reynolds 2009; Scourfield and Lewinson 2016; Williams 2009; Williams et al. 2013).

From an intersectional perspective, providing support to Sam's parents will honour their assets and strengths, while most importantly avoiding a deficit approach that focuses only on problems and deficiencies; being able to engage and communicate with families is an essential part of any assessment, as is being cognisant of the needs and assets of families to avoid a deficit model (Bernard and Thomas 2016). In essence, an intersectional approach offers some tools to facilitate a strengths-based model of working with this family, giving greater visibility to aspects of family life that can be enhanced to support Sam. Even so, practitioners must keep in mind that whilst the parents' religious beliefs can strengthen family relationships, it is also important to be cognisant of the ways that religious beliefs may enable parental practices that pose a risk to children (Bernard 2019). Thus, an intersectional perspective is particularly important for enabling reflective thinking to gain rich insights into the nuances of familial relationships when there are 'layers of complexities of multiple, competing, fluid and intersecting identities' (Gringeri et al. 2010, 394). Intersectionality as an analytical concept can therefore help to unpack the specificity of experiences in the family history and functioning as it offers the means to interrogate some of the issues framing family contexts and most notably, the person-in environment, to understand the family and environmental factors at the macro social-structural level (Nadan et al. 2015).

Of particular relevance is intersectionality's capacity for fostering professional curiosity. Thus, an argument can be made that an intersectional lens encourages social workers to be professionally curious because it opens up possibilities for understanding how sources of multiple inequalities intersect to impact children and their families' circumstances. To this end, intersectionality offers the possibilities to disentangle the multiple interlocking spheres that intersect and overlap for children and their families.

Conclusion

This chapter has explored ways in which intersectionality can provide a conceptual framework to aid assessments of children's and families' circumstances in situations where there are concerns about the safety and welfare of children. It drew on a case study to show how the conceptual tools of intersectionality can be employed to shed light on multiple identities and subjective experiences in child welfare encounters. In particular, the chapter highlighted how, through an intersectional lens, social workers can engage effectively with the complex issues that arise for children and their families when there are safeguarding concerns. The main argument of the chapter is that intersectionality can serve as a vehicle to help social workers unpick the entanglements of issues that are often involved when making assessments of risks and needs with families from diverse racial and religious backgrounds. An intersectionality approach provides a framework that can be used alongside the

Assessment Triangle (Department of Health 2000) to facilitate more nuanced appreciation of the developmental needs of minority ethnic children, parenting capacity and the family and environmental factors that impact their lived experiences. The central point, then, is that employing intersectionality elucidates how important it is for practitioners to think themselves into the frame of reference of families in order to bring a structural understanding of the social problems that impact families' lived experiences. In crucial ways, then, intersectionality provides an overarching framework to enrich social workers' understandings of how interlocking oppressions manifest to structure the everyday experiences of children and families in need of social work support.

Key points

- Intersectionality shifts attention away from individualising social problems and
- Intersectionality encourages an appreciation of how structural inequalities impact the lived experiences of diverse groups of children and families.
- An intersectional framework offers some tools to enable nuanced conversations about power, race, gender, and class oppression in situations where there are concerns about the safety and welfare of vulnerable children.
- Intersectionality creates a critical framework that can facilitate strengths-based orientation to help engage resistant families in child protection work.

Reflective questions

- How might intersectionality influence the questions you ask about child maltreatment?

- How might you integrate an intersectional lens into your work as a social worker?
- How can you open up discussions around intersectionality in individual and group supervision?

References

Adams, Robert, Lena Dominelli, and Malcolm Payne. 2009. *Social Work: Themes, Issues and Critical Debates*, 3rd edn. Basingstoke: Palgrave Macmillan.

Alijah, Zahrah, and Khatidja Chantler. 2015. Forced marriage is a child protection matter. In *Domestic Violence and Protecting Children: New Thinking and Approaches*, eds. Nicky Stanley and Cathy Humphreys, 97–111. London: Jessica Kingsley.

Atkin, Annabelle L., and Hyung Chol Yoo. 2019. Familial racial-ethnic socialization of multiracial American youth: A systematic review of the literature with MultiCrit, *Development Review 53*: https://doi.org/10.1016/j.dr.2019.100869.

Barn, Ravinder, and Derek Kirton. 2015. Child welfare and migrant families and children: A case study of England. In *Child Welfare Systems and Migrant Children: A Cross Country Study of Policies and Practice*, eds. Ravinder Barn, Križ Katrin, Pösö Tarja, and Skivenes Marit, 199–219. Oxford and New York: Oxford University Press.

Beckett, Helen. Isabelle Brodie, Fiona Factor, Margaret Melrose, Jenny Pearce, John Pitts, Lucie Shuker and Camille Warrington. 2013. It's wrong but you get used to it: A qualitative study of gang-associated sexual violence towards, and sexual exploitation of, young people in England. London: Office of the Children's Commissioner.

Bernard, Claudia. 2013. Black feminist thinking, black mothers, and child sexual abuse. In *Failure to Protect: Moving Beyond Gendered Responses*, eds. Susan Strega, Julia Krane, Simon Lapierre, Cathy Richardson, and Rosemary Carlton, 107–124. Winnipeg: Fernwood.

Bernard, Claudia. 2019. Working with cultural and religious diversity. In *The Child's World*, 3rd edn., eds. Jan Horwath and Dendy Platt, 649–665. London: Jessica Kingsley.

Bernard, Claudia, and Anna Gupta. 2008. Black African children and the child protection system, *British Journal of Social Work* 38 (3): 476–492.

Bernard, Claudia and Perlita Harris. 2019. Serious case reviews: The lived experience of black children. *Child and Family Social Work* 24 (2): 24, 256–263.

Bernard, Claudia, and Shantel Thomas. 2016. Risk and safety: A strengths-based perspective in working with black families when there are safeguarding concerns. In *Social Work in a Diverse Society: Transformative Practice with Black and Ethnic Minority Individuals and Communities*, eds. Charlotte Williams and Mekada Graham, 59–74. Bristol: Policy Press.

Bokhari, Farrah. 2008. Falling through the gaps: Safeguarding children trafficked into the UK. *Children and Society* 22 (3): 201–211.

Briggs, Stephen, and Andrew Whittaker. 2018. Protecting children from faith-based abuse through accusations of witchcraft and spirit possession: Understanding contexts and informing practice. *The British Journal of Social Work* 48 (8): 2157–2175,

Bywaters, Paul, Geraldine Brady, Tim Sparks, and Elizabeth Bos. 2016. Inequalities in child welfare intervention rates: The intersection of deprivation and identity. *Child and Family Social Work* 21 (4): 452–463.

Clayton, Sue, Anna Gupta, and Katie Willis. 2019. *Unaccompanied Young Migrants: Identity, Care and Justice.* Bristol: Policy Press.

Connelly, Elaine, Nina Murray, Helen Baillot, and Natasha Howard. 2018. Missing from the debate? A qualitative study exploring the role of communities within interventions to address female genital mutilation in Europe. *BMJ Open* 8 (6), doi:10.1136/bmjopen-2017-021430.

Costello, Susie, Marjorie Quinn, Allison Tatchell, Lynne Jordan, and Koula Neophytou. 2015. In the best interests of the child: Preventing female genital cutting (FGC). *British Journal of Social Work* 45 (4): 1259–1276.

Davis, Linda and Julia Krane. 1997. Shaking the legacy of mother blaming: No easy task for child welfare. *Journal of Progressive Human Services* 7 (2): 3–22.

Department for Education. 2012. National action plan to tackle child abuse linked to faith or belief. Available at: https://assets.publishing.service.gov.uk › file › Act. Accessed 18 May 2018.

Department of Health. 2000. *Assessing Children in Need and Their Families: Practice Guidance*. London: Stationery Office.

Ehntholt, Kimberly A., David Trickey, Jean Harris Hendriks, Hannah Chambers, Mark Scott, and William Yule. 2018. Mental health of unaccompanied asylum-seeking adolescents previously held in British detention centres. *Clinical Child Psychology and Psychiatry* 23 (2): 238–257.

Featherstone, Brid. 2010. Writing fathers in but mothers out!!! *Critical Social Policy* 30 (2): 208–224.

Featherstone, Brid, Anna Gupta, Kate Morris, and Sue White. 2018. *Protecting Children: A Social Model*. Bristol: Policy Press.

Featherstone, Brid, Sue White, and Kate Morris. 2014. *Re-imagining Child Protection: Towards Humane Social Work with Families*. Bristol: Policy Press.

Firmin, Carlene. 2018. Contextual risk, individualised responses: An assessment of safeguarding responses to nine cases of peer-on-peer abuse. *Child Abuse Review* 27 (1): 42–57.

Firmin, Carlene, Camille Warrington, and Jenny Pearce. 2016. Sexual exploitation and its impact on developing sexualities and sexual relationships: The need for contextual social work intervention. *British Journal of Social Work* 46 (8): 2318–2337.

Gilmour, Lynn, Nicola Ring, and Margaret Maxwell. 2019. Review: The views and experiences of suicidal children and young people of mental health support services: A meta-ethnography. *Child and Adolescent Mental Health* 24 (3): 217–229.

Gregor, Claire, Helen Hingley-Jones, and Sarah Davidson. 2015. Understanding the experience of parents of pre-pubescent children with gender identity issues. *Child and Adolescence Social Work Journal* 32 (3): 237–246.

Gringeri E. Christina, Stéphanie Wahab and Ben Anderson-Nathe. 2010. What makes it feminist? Mapping the landscape of feminist social work research. *Affilia: Journal of Women and Social Work* 25 (4): 390–405.

Gupta, Anna. 2016. Forced marriage as a safeguarding issue. In *Safeguarding Black Children: Good Practice in Child Protection*, eds. Claudia Bernard and Perlita Harris, 200–215. London: Jessica Kingsley.

Gupta, Anna, and Brid Featherstone. 2016. What about my dad? Black fathers and the child protection system. *Critical and Radical Social Work* 4 (1): 77–91.

Harris, Perlita. 2016. Safeguarding black children from female genital mutilation. In *Safeguarding Black Children: Good Practice in Child Protection*, eds. Claudia Bernard and Perlita Harris, 216–238. London: Jessica Kingsley.

HM Government. 1989. *The Children Act 1989*. London: Stationery Office.

HM Government. 2018. *Working Together to Safeguard Children: A Guide to Interagency Working to Safeguard and Promote the Welfare of Children*. London: Stationery Office.

Keating, Frank. 2016. Racialized communities, producing madness and dangerousness. *Intersectionalities* 5 (3): 173–185.

Keating, Frank. 2019. Understanding race and ethnicity in mental health. In *Understanding 'Race' and Ethnicity: Theory, History, Policy and Practice*, 2nd edn., eds. Sangeeta Chattoo, Karl Atkin, Gary Craig, and Ronny Flynn, 201–226. Bristol: Policy Press.

Keddell, Emily, and Ian Hyslop. 2019. Ethnic inequalities in child welfare: The role of practitioner risk perceptions. *Child and Family Social Work* 24 (4), 409–420.

Krumer-Nevo, Michal, Adva Berkovitz-Romano, and Michal Komem. 2015. The study of girls in social work: Major discourses and feminist ideas. *Journal of Social Work*, 15 (4): 425–446.

Mattsson, Tina. 2014. Intersectionality as a useful tool: Anti-oppressive social work and critical reflection. *Affilia* 29 (1): 8–17.

McDonnell, Christina G., Andrea D. Boan, Catherine C. Bradley, Kristen D. Seay, Jane M. Charles, and Laura A. Carpenter. 2018. Child maltreatment in autism spectrum disorder and intellectual disability: Results from a population-based sample. *The Journal of Child Psychology and Psychiatry* 60 (5): 576–584.

McLean, Kate C., Jennifer P. Lilgendahl, Chelsea Fordham, Elizabeth Alpert, Emma Marsden, Kathryn Szymanowski, and Dan P.

McAdams. 2017. Identity development in cultural context: The role of deviating from master narratives. *Journal of Personality* 86 (4): 631–651.

McLeigh, Jill D. 2013. Protecting children in the context of international migration. *Child Abuse and Neglect* 37 (12): 1056–1068.

Mehrotra, Gita. 2010. Toward a continuum of intersectionality theorizing for feminist social work scholarship. *Affilia* 25 (4): 417–430.

Morris, Kate, Will Mason, Paul Bywaters, Brid Featherstone, Brigid Daniel, Geraldine Brady, Lisa Bunting, Jade Hooper, Nughmana Mirza, Jonathan Scourfield, and Calum Webb. 2018. Social work, poverty, and child welfare interventions. *Child and Family Social Work* 23 (3): 364–372.

Murphy, Yvette, Valerie Hunt, Anna M. Zajicek, Adele N. Norris, and Leah Hamilton. 2009. *Incorporating Intersectionality in Social Work Practice, Research, Policy and Education.* Washington, DC: NASW.

Nadan, Yochay, James C. Spilsbury, Jill E. Korbin. 2015. Culture and context in understanding child maltreatment: Contributions of intersectionality and neighborhood-based research. *Child Abuse and Neglect* 41: 40–48.

Ni Raghallaigh, Muireann. 2014. The causes of mistrust amongst asylum seekers and refugees: Insights from research with unaccompanied asylum-seeking minors living in the Republic of Ireland. *Journal of Refugee Studies* 27 (1): 82–100.

Owen, Charlie, and June Statham. 2009. Disproportionality in child welfare: The prevalence of black and minority ethnic children within the 'looked after' and 'children in need' populations and on child protection registers in England. London: Institute of Education.

Reynolds, Tracey. 2009. Exploring the absent/present dilemma: Black fathers, family relationships, and social capital in Britain. *The Annals of the American Academy of Political and Social Science* 624 (1): 12–28.

Ruch, Gillian. 2014. 'Helping children is a human process': Researching the challenges social workers face in communicating with children. *The British Journal of Social Work* 44 (8): 2145–2162.

Scourfield, Jonathan and Elizabeth Lewinson. 2016. Engaging black fathers in child protection services. In *Safeguarding Black*

Children: Good Practice in Child Protection, eds. Claudia Bernard and Perlita Harris, 165–176. London: Jessica Kingsley.

Selwyn, Julie, David Quinton, Perlita Harris, Dinithi Wijedasa, Shameem Nawaz, and Marsha Wood. 2010. *Pathways to Permanence for Black, Asian and Mixed Ethnicity Children: Dilemmas, Decision-Making and Outcomes*. London: Turnaround.

Shannon, Patrick, and Christine Tappan. 2011. A qualitative analysis of child protective services practice with children with developmental disabilities. *Children and Youth Services Review* 33 (9): 1469–1475.

Stalker, Kirsten and Katharine McArthur. 2012. Child abuse, child protection and disabled children: A review of recent research. *Child Abuse Review*, 21 (1): 24–40.

Stobart, Eleanor. 2006. *Child Abuse Linked to Accusation of 'Possession' and 'Witchcraft'*. London: DfES.

Strier, Roni, Guy Feldman and Corey Shdaimah. 2012. The construction of social class in social work education: A study of introductory textbooks. *Journal of Teaching in Social Work* 32 (4): 406–420.

Tait, Audrey and Helen Wosu. 2019. Securing effective communication with children and young people. In *The Child's World*, 3rd edn., eds. Jan Horwath and Dendy Platt, 106–120. London: Jessica Kingsley.

Tatum, Beverly D. 2004. Family life and school experience: Factors in the racial identity development of black youth in white communities. *Journal of Social Issues*, 60 (1): 117–135.

Tedam, Prospera. 2016. Safeguarding children linked to witchcraft. In *Safeguarding Black Children: Good Practice in Child Protection*, eds. Claudia Bernard and Perlita Harris, 216–239. London: Jessica Kingsley.

Tedam, Prospera, and Awura Adjoa, A. 2017. *The W Word: Witchcraft Labelling and Child Safeguarding in Social Work Practice*. St Albans: Critical Publishing Ltd.

Thorne, Barrie. 2004. Theorising age and other differences. *Childhood* 11 (4): 403–408.

Tilbury, Clare, and June Thoburn. 2009. Using racial disproportionality and disparity indicators to measure child welfare outcomes. *Children and Youth Services Review* 31 (10): 1101–1106.

Tizard, Barbara, and Ann Phoenix. 1995. The identity of mixed parentage adolescents. *The Journal of Child Psychology and Psychiatry and Allied Disciplines* 36 (8): 1399–1410.

Westwood, Joanne. 2016. Safeguarding unaccompanied asylum-seeking children. In *Safeguarding Black Children: Good Practice in Child Protection*, eds. Claudia Bernard and Perlita Harris, 239–252. London: Jessica Kingsley.

Williams, Robert. 2009. Masculinities and vulnerability: The solitary discourses and practices of African-Caribbean and white working-class fathers. *Men and Masculinities* 11 (4): 441–461.

Williams, Robert, Alistair Hewison, Stuart Wildman, and Carolyn Roskell. 2013. Changing fatherhood: An exploratory qualitative study with African and African Caribbean men in England. *Children and Society* 27 (2): 92–103.

4 Intersectionality in mental health social work

This chapter applies intersectional thinking to issues arising for black and minority ethnic users of mental health services. The argument I make here is that intersectionality is a useful framework because it provides ways for understanding how intersecting inequalities overlap and interweave for users who experience oppression in multifaceted ways. The aim is to deepen understandings of lived experiences when there are interplays of various forms of inequalities that contribute to how mental ill-health is experienced and responded to. I begin by sketching some of the issues that contribute to mental health problems in racialised contexts, before moving on to draw on case examples to explore how intersectionality can be used in practices and interventions. The chapter concludes by considering how intersectional thinking can enhance capacity for relationship-based practice with users of mental health services.

Mental health in a racialised context

It is commonly recognised that black and minority ethnic communities are disproportionately affected by mental health (Barnett et al. 2019; Fernando 2017; Gajwani et al. 2016; Grey et al. 2013; Keating et al. 2019; Lane et al. 2011; Synergi Collaborative Centre 2018). Mental health researchers are careful to point out that there are social drivers of health disparities which lead to the over-representation of black and minority ethnic groups in the mental health system (Bignall et al. 2019; Fernando 2010; Grey et al. 2013; Keating et al. 2019; Keating and Brown 2016; Tang 2017). Indeed, a number of researchers have centred racism as a key determinant of mental health and suggest that black people in particular are much more likely to be diagnosed with mental health problems than anyone else in the UK

DOI: 10.4324/9780429467288-4

(Bhui et al. 2018; Grey et al. 2013; Mental Health Foundation 2020). It has also been emphasised that social and contextual factors such as underlying structural inequalities, socio-economic deprivation, and discrimination leave black and minority ethnic people, who are disproportionately from lower socio-economic backgrounds, at greater risks of developing mental health problems (Bhui et al. 2018; Grey et al. 2013; Wallace 2016). A number of arguments have been made about the ways that inadequate and inappropriate services result in the worst mental health outcomes for black and minority ethnic groups (Keating et al. 2019; Wilson et al. 2009). For example, research has consistently reported that black and minority ethnic groups most frequently encounter immensely inadequate support in the system and experience poor assessments and intervention (Cudjoe et al. 2019; Fernando 2010; Hickson et al. 2017; Linton and Walcott 2018; Memon et al. 2016).

It has been shown that black and minority ethnic people are much more likely to receive crisis mental care and are less likely to receive talking therapies in their recovery (Fernando 2017; Gajwani et al. 2016). Furthermore, it has been well documented that black and minority ethnic groups are more likely to be detained on a compulsory basis, are admitted through the criminal justice system route, and stay longer in detention (Barnett et al. 2019; Byrne et al. 2020; Gajwani et al. 2016; Morgan et al. 2004; Singh et al. 2007). Research revealed that the Mental Health Act (1983) is used in a coercive and controlling ways to admit and detain people from black and minority ethnic backgrounds (Barnett et al. 2019; Byrne et al. 2020; Gajwani et al. 2016). Of particular interest are the disproportionate numbers of black and minority people who experience the harsher end of the mental health system, leading some to reflect on the powerful role of institutional racism within the system (Fernando 2017; Kim et al. 2020; Memon et al. 2016). With this in mind, the Mental Health Act Review set out to examine the concerns raised about the rising number of detentions, the racial disparity in the use of the Act, and that attacks on human rights and dignity were being disregarded (Department of Health 2019). A key recommendation of the Review was the urgent need to address the ethnic and cultural needs of service users from black and minority ethnic backgrounds.

Intersecting multiple oppressions

Although it can be argued that black and minority ethnic men and women share the commonalities of race-related stressors, as well as poor support in the mental health services, there are some qualitative differences in experiences (Adkison-Bradley et al. 2009; Keating 2020; Morgan et al. 2004). However, when you bring gender into central view, what is illuminated is that, as well as experiencing racial stressors, minoritised women face some added challenges that significantly contribute to their susceptibility to poor mental health outcomes (Chantler 2012; Memon et al. 2016; Sellers et al. 2006; Wilson 2001). For example, it has been highlighted that women from minority backgrounds experience multiple forms of gender-based violence, such as domestic abuse, sexual violence, sexual exploitation, forced marriage, and female genital mutilation, which heighten risks to chronic stress, depression, anxiety, and other mental health problems (Ashley 2014; Chantler et al. 2009; Chantler and Gangoli 2009; Gangoli and Chantler 2009; Memon et al. 2016; Wilson 2001). Added to such factors are expectations of race loyalty, which places women in a precarious position to not speak about private 'family business' in public—often referred to as 'airing dirty linen in public'. Furthermore, research into maternal mental illness has noted that black and minority ethnic women's needs are often not understood or overlooked by health professionals (Anand and Cochrane 2005; Edge et al. 2004; Wilson 2001). For instance, research into perinatal depression among black women of Caribbean descent found that there was often a failure by health professionals to identify and diagnose maternal depressive symptoms (Edge et al. 2004). Likewise, research into South Asian women's experiences of mental ill-health elucidates that there are elevated levels of depression, suicide, parasuicide, self-harm, and eating disorders (Anand and Cochrane 2005). Research also reveals that linkages of cultural and religious practices are influential in how mental ill-health is understood and given expression as well as in framing coping strategies and help-seeking behaviours (Anand and Cochrane 2005; Dein and Illaiee 2013; Littlewood and Dien 2013; Sellers et al. 2006).

Additionally, as well as race and gender inequalities, there are other intersecting identities, such as age, sexuality, disability, religion, and immigration status, that combine to add further layers of complexities. Therefore, black and minority ethnic women face a situation where different sources of inequality will coalesce to affect the situational contexts of their mental health, their experiences markedly different if they are older, disabled, lesbian or trans, a refugee or asylum seeker, for example.

All in all, these insights offer an alternative understanding of the mental health issues that manifest for diverse groups of black and minority ethnic women. An understanding of these issues is important for recognising how invisible features of oppression shore up unique experiences for multiply oppressed women in the mental health system (Chantler 2012; Mehrotra 2010; Wilson, 2001).

Racial trauma and mental health

Antiracist scholarship proposes that racial trauma is an important category of risk for black and minority ethnic people's psychological well-being and mental health (Bryant-Davis and Ocampo 2005; Chakraborty et al. 2009; Chakraborty et al. 2013; Wallace et al. 2016). A number of scholars cite racism in our society, both individual and institutionalised, as the root cause of adverse psychological consequences for black people that leads to poor mental health (Pierce 1974; Sue et al. 2007; Williams et al. 2018). Racial trauma can result from major experiences of racism such as discrimination in the workplace, or as a result of hate crimes such as racial attacks, vicarious experiences of race-related violence, or can result from an accumulation of small everyday occurrences of discrimination, and what is generally referred to as microaggressions; that is, the frequent race encounters that impart key hostile, devaluing, and derogatory messages to black and minority ethnic people (Bryant-Davis and Ocampo 2006; Miller and Vittrup 2020; Williams et al. 2018). As described by Comas-Díaz (2016), racialised gendered microaggressions operate at various points of intersection to cause nuanced racial wounds for black and minority ethnic women, thus compounding their mental health challenges. This view is supported by findings that challenge us to think about what Alleyne (2005, 288) refers to as invisible injuries and black identity wounding. Indeed, the term racial battle fatigue was originally conceptualised to understand the social and psychological stressors resulting from everyday racism experienced by black people (Smith et al. 2007). In essence, recognising the psychological toll of racism is essential for a deeper understanding of the impact of racial trauma on black and minority ethnic people's lived experiences of mental health.

The mental health needs of black and minority ethnic children and young people

Recent focus on the mental health needs of young people has illuminated that there are particular concerns about the experiences of Black and minority ethnic children and young people (Bécares et al. 2015; Gutman et al. 2015; Mhemooda and Joughin 2004; Roe 2018). In particular, concerns have been raised about the over-representation of Black and minority ethnic children and young people in the mental health system (Gilburt 2018; Khan et al. 2017; Malek and Joughin 2004). Research has demonstrated that multiple adverse childhood experiences, including peer-on-peer violence, living in gang affected neighbourhoods, socio-economic disadvantage, domestic violence, and intrafamilial abuse and neglect put black and minority ethnic children and young people at greater risk of developing mental health problems (Goodman et al. 2008; Keating and Brown, 2016; Mental Health Foundation 2018; NHS Digital 2005). We also know that black children, who are disproportionately in the looked after system, are also at increased risk of developing mental health problems (Richardson and Joughin 2000). It has also been shown that children who come into the care system are more likely to have suffered abuse and neglect, and to have been exposed to parents' problematic use of alcohol and drugs, which increases their risks of developing mental health problems over the life course (Ford et al. 2007; Kysar-Moon 2020; McAuley and Young 2006; Stanley et al. 2005). We also know from research evidence that a high proportion of mental disorders take root in childhood, and most long-term mental health problems begin in early teens (Department of Health 2011). Hence, it is crucial to understand how intrafamilial and extrafamilial factors intersect to impact the mental health of black and minority ethnic children. Even more importantly, it must be stressed that pre-existing racial disadvantages are being compounded by mental health problems for black and minority ethnic children. With these concerns in mind, in the challenging world of mental health practice the locus of attention must be on the multiple adverse childhood experiences that increase their risks to mental health problems.

Intersectionality: A challenge for mental health social work

Against this background, how can intersectional thinking be applied in mental health social work? One important factor here is the crucial context for understanding the mental health experiences of black and minority ethnic groups. For social work practice in mental health, intersectionality offers an effective tool for meaning-making between social workers and mental health service users. Specifically, intersectional thinking can help social workers to co-construct understanding with users of mental health services of their lived experiences. As a number of commentators remind us, when a person with multiple stigmatised identities receives a mental health diagnosis, it adds another layer of stigma to an already undervalued identity (Carr 2014; Keating 2016; Lane et al. 2011). In particular, social workers need to better appreciate how social inequalities frame the lives of the individuals they are working with to more effectively engage with their lived realities and experiences (Synergi Collaborative Centre 2018).

Crucially, intersectionality encourages social workers to pay critical attention to the instrumental role that inequalities play in amplifying vulnerability to mental health problems for people from black and minority ethnic backgrounds (Graham 2007; Fernando and Keating 2009; Keating 2016; Keating and Brown 2016). What is noteworthy here is that intersectionality assists in asking the thorny questions for a more nuanced consideration of different forms of discrimination experienced by individuals with marginalised intersecting identities (Karban 2017; Keating 2007; Robinson et al. 2013; Tang 2017). In this sense, an intersectional lens provides a useful framing for dissecting how multiple and shifting identities come together to give rise to the myriad challenges for black and minority ethnic groups in the mental health system.

My main point here is that intersectionality has something distinctive to offer. Firstly, it allows social workers to engage in the reflective work that is necessary for critiquing the medical and social perspectives that are put forward to explain mental illness (Bland et al. 2009). Secondly, it enables social workers to interrogate the toxic effects that racism and disadvantage have on the well-being and mental health of black and minority ethnic people and in so doing centres a social justice stance in their interventions. As Keating (2016) indicates, in mental health social work, an intersectional interpretive perspective can help social workers develop a critical lens for probing into experiences that are rooted in systemic inequalities to develop anti-oppressive practices and interventions. In other words, an intersectional approach offers the potential for deepening understandings of the multiple barriers faced by individuals from disadvantaged backgrounds who are at greater risk of only experiencing the control aspects of mental health services.

It is against this background that intersectionality as an explanatory tool can be employed to make sense of the multiple factors that create the conditions for black people's vulnerability to mental health problems. For illustrative purposes, I will now use a case vignette to show how intersectional ideas can be applied to make sense of the care and mental health support needs of vulnerable service users.

Case study: Mr A

Mr A is a 33-year-old black British man of African heritage. He has a history of mental illness. He first came to the attention of mental health services at the age of 27 when he was detained under the Mental Health Act 1983. At that time, his mother took him to the Accident and Emergency department of his local hospital because he was experiencing symptoms of psychosis and expressed suicidal ideation. He had reportedly 'walked into her bedroom, and said he was hearing voices, was under demonic attack and the demons wanted to kill him'. He was thus sectioned under the Mental Health Act and detained in a psychiatric hospital for one month. When he was discharged from hospital, he was referred to the Community Mental Health Team (CMHT), but Mr A struggled to keep appointments and mental health services failed to meaningfully engage him in the services.

Last week, a family member became worried about Mr A, whose mental health had deteriorated, and thus contacted mental health services expressing serious concerns about his recent change in mood and behaviour. This family member felt that his mental health was deteriorating, and they were 'scared to be alone with him'. There were also concerns about his substance misuse and the impact it was having. At the time of the referral, he was living alone in what used to be the family home. His mother and sister had recently been rehoused due to the council downsizing policy and Mr A therefore remained an 'unauthorised occupant' with the council intent to seek possession, leaving Mr A at risk of homelessness. Mr A works in a supermarket and in his spare time volunteers as a football coach to a local team. In relation to his current family situation, little is known about his broader family history and social support networks. He experienced a difficult childhood and had been a looked after child, having spent significant periods of his childhood in and out of the care system. In the past, he has expressed that there was discord between him and his mother, and that he experienced her involvement in his life as an intrusion.

In response to this referral, the Approved Mental Health Professional (AMHP) made several attempts to see Mr A, but he has not responded to letters or messages left and is perceived by CMHT as being very resistant to engaging with them. His inaction in responding to letters/messages left and his previous mistrust in engaging with mental health services suggests that it is unlikely he will voluntarily agree to accept the help that he needs. An application was therefore made to the Court under S135 (1) of the Mental Health Act 1983 for Mr A to be removed to a place of safety. Thus, on the day of the referral an AMPH, the police, S12 Doctor and Ambulance service went to Mr A's home to take him to a place of safety for a Mental Health Act Assessment.

Before considering how intersectionality can be used as an analytical lens for a more comprehensive understanding of Mr A's needs, let me briefly sketch some issues that are important to keep in mind. First and foremost, preserving the dignity and worth of Mr A should be uppermost in the Mental Health Act assessment that is carried out. As a starting point, the social worker will need to ascertain to what extent Mr A is cognisant of what is happening in relation to his rights and choices, such as reasons for the professionals' presence, as well as their actions and the implications for his care and treatment. Mr A essentially has to demonstrate mental capacity through his understanding and retention of the information he is provided with about the legal basis for their intervention (Mental Capacity Act 2005). Moreover, an important issue to keep in mind is that he may be discouraged from engaging with the services because of a mistrust of the system as sources of help, due to his past experiences. Additionally, in terms of undertaking assessments of risk, the decisions that social workers have to make in these kinds of situations are difficult and challenging and often there are no easy answers (Gilburt 2021). As such, the social worker must respect Mr A's right to autonomy to make decisions for himself, but at the same time ensure that he has the ability to advocate for himself and, most importantly, that his behaviour does not cause harm to himself or other people (BASW 2014) In other words, the social worker has to respond with respect and humility to support, protect, and empower, all at the same time (BASW 2014). It would seem presently that what Mr A might consider to be in his best interest may be in conflict with what the social worker thinks is best for his well-being and safety. This conundrum throws up many challenges that the social worker will have to navigate, to respond to Mr A in his troubling circumstances, to establish what kinds of support will be helpful for him. Therefore, building a rapport with Mr A is going to be critical to facilitate a relational approach (Keating 2020).

What, then, can intersectionality contribute? In this case example, we can see that a number of salient factors interact and intersect to amplify Mr A's vulnerabilities; utilising intersectionality invites the social worker to look more deeply at the particularities of Mr A's lived experiences (Keating 2016). Starting from an intersectional perspective essentially provides a way of thinking that urges the social worker to critically reflect on their own values, beliefs, attitudes, and behaviours to consider how these sit within some of the core social work values of respect for equality, worth and dignity (BASW 2014). An intersectional approach will support the social worker to be better prepared for helping Mr A to fully engage with the services. By employing an intersectional framework, the social worker can draw on its key concepts of social inequalities, power, oppression, and social justice as a lens from which to forefront the salient issues that will need to be considered for developing supportive care that is responsive to Mr A's multifaceted needs (Hill Collins 2019). In essence, an intersectional perspective has the potential to offer ways to assess the particulars of Mr A's everyday life that forms the backdrop for the emotional and psychological distress he is currently experiencing. Ultimately, to meaningfully engage and build a relationship with Mr A will require entering into conversations with him to understand how he embodies his identity as a black man. Further, we cannot make assumptions about what his hopes, dreams, and future aspirations may be, and these are important things to keep an open mind about during the assessment. The social worker must therefore be proactive in involving an Independent Mental Health Advocate (IMHA) service as an additional safeguard for Mr A to ensure that his rights are respected and adequately represented in the decisions that are taken about his care and treatment. An intersectional approach thus helps the social worker to be attuned to how multiple inequalities and power imbalances manifest to ensure that Mr A has the culturally appropriate advocacy and support that will enable his voice to be heard (Fernando 2017; Keating 2016; Newbigging et al. 2013).

In respect to getting a contextualised understanding of Mr A's needs, drawing on intersectionality's core constructs of oppression and inequalities will highlight the various disadvantage that play a crucial role in shaping his experiences. For example, intersectionality offers an important interpretive lens to understand how Mr A's complex and overlapping needs are impacted by a wide range of adversities including substance misuse, as well as structural factors such as poverty and insecure housing, all of which increase the risk of mental health problems. Given these aspects, an intersectional analysis can help to untangle the dynamic interaction of factors that manifest for Mr A in his experience of the mental health system. Hence, the application of intersectionality can illuminate the social injustices that compound and exacerbate Mr A's mental health problems. In this way, an intersectional understanding allows the social worker to move away from a biomedical model of mental health, and to instead attend to the interlocking aspects of race, gender, and social class that negatively influence Mr A's experience of mental ill health in order to provide supportive care. What intersectionality allows us to do is to maintain a critical stance in order to delve into how the psychosocial stressors take a toll on Mr A's physical and mental well-being.

Another important benefit of an intersectional approach is that it enables consideration of how Mr A is impacted by adverse childhood experiences. Take, for example, that Mr A has spent most of his childhood in and out of the care system, which would suggest that he experienced childhood adversities, and we know from available evidence that care-experienced young people have increased risk of developing mental health problems in later life (Richardson and Joughin 2000). These factors are important to consider for understanding the adverse psychological marks that have affected Mr A. Specifically, engaging with these issues can also give greater context to Mr A's experiences and the nuances of his story in order to provide support that is timely to meaningfully engage him in mental health services. An intersectional analysis therefore has a lot to offer for making space to explore the psychosocial factors that have an impact on his experience of mental ill-health in a much more nuanced way.

Moreover, taking an intersectional approach can yield insights into how systematic racism intersects with other forms of disadvantage that impact Mr A's lived experiences. Additionally, as previously mentioned, disproportionate representation and disparate treatment means that black men like Mr A have poor outcomes in the mental health system because they are less likely to get the help that they need (Borschmann et al. 2010). For example, it has long been acknowledged that racial bias is a major factor in making black men like Mr A more likely to come into contact with mental services through the police under section 136 of the Mental Health Act (Barnett et al. 2019; Walker 2020). Intersectionality can therefore offer important new insights of how these compounding factors may have accelerated Mr A's mental health problems, presenting him with unique challenges. Intersectionality, then, can enable an interrogation of the critical role that race plays in fostering deep-rooted racial stereotypes about the 'dangerous black man' myth that results in men like Mr A being treated more harshly in the mental health system (Bhui et al. 2018; Fernando 2017; Keating 2016; Keating et al. 2019; Walker 2020). Using this perspective therefore helps to connect Mr A's personal experiences to structural inequalities for making sense of the subtle race-related stressors that impact him (Wilson 2009). In short, intervention based on intersectional ideas opens the way for recognising the racialised gendered elements that are at the core of Mr A's mental health experiences to consider which practices will help to achieve the best possible outcomes for him.

Clearly, intersectionality raises crucial questions about the interconnectedness of systems of oppression, thus enabling us to have a more nuanced understanding of Mr A's help-seeking behaviour and ability to ask for and receive help. Likewise, an intersectional lens will enable the social worker to consider why he may not engage with or may disengage from services (Wilson 2009). As such, the benefit of intersectionality is that it offers crucial insights into the specificities of Mr A's mental health experiences, to shed light on the barriers for him to access good care and support. Additionally, because empowerment is a core tenet of intersectionality, it therefore facilitates a social justice-oriented perspective of Mr A's situation to recognise and affirm his value and strengths (Hill Collins 2019). Thus, central to an intersectional approach is the mechanism to ensure that a rights-based and relational approach will be at the centre of Mr A's assessment. Intersectionality can therefore offer a useful lens for increasing our understandings of the manifold ways that Mr A's experiences need to be understood in the broader social context of his life (Keating 2020). More importantly, intersectionality brings to the forefront that Mr A is at the sharpest end of inequalities and is confronted with some distinctive challenges. At the same time, using intersectionality as a tool offers a critical perspective of the hurdles Mr A has to navigate to access and engage with services. The distinguishing feature of intersectionality is that its key aims are to interrogate how different forms of oppression overlap, therefore it affords opportunities to develop strengths-based interventions with service users like Mr A to develop practice that is grounded in social justice principles.

Conclusion

This chapter has endeavoured to look at some of the ways intersectional thinking can be employed to analyse situations in mental health care. I have highlighted the debates about racial and ethnic disparities in the mental health services and illuminated how race inequality in particular intersects with gender, socio-economic status, age, and factors such as the cultural context to play a significant role in influencing the route through which people from black and minority ethnic backgrounds enter the mental health system. As I have argued throughout this chapter, intersectionality can help to shines a light on the barriers that people from racial minority backgrounds face in the mental health system. Intersectionality theory, then, offers a lens through which social workers can engage effectively with the complex issues involving stigma, cultural barriers and systemic inequalities that compound experiences of mental health care and support. With the use of a case vignette, I have illustrated some ways the conceptual tools of intersectionality can be engaged to illuminate the complex layers of experiences in mental health cases. Importantly, an intersectional approach can help social workers attend to the complexity of issues that is often deeply enmeshed when making assessments of risks and safety in mental health situations. In essence, an intersectional approach provides a critical reflexive framework that practitioners can use alongside practice frameworks such as a trauma-informed approaches, or strengths-based approaches, to conduct more effective assessments of the lived experiences of vulnerability for users of mental health services from marginalised backgrounds. Finally, intersectionality provides a vantage point to pay critical attention to how interlocking oppressions manifest in mental health social work.

Key points

- Intersectionality, as an interpretive tool, can help to interrogate multiple disadvantages in mental health for developing anti-oppressive practice.
- Intersectionality starts from the premise of a social justice orientation; therefore, it offers rich opportunities for learning about the

contexts of lived experiences for culturally diverse groups in the mental health system.

- An intersectional perspective invites social workers to meaningfully engage with the effects of discrimination, power, and oppression in mental health social work.

Reflective questions

- How can intersectionality help us to understand the full extent of risks and needs for marginalised groups requiring mental health care and support?
- In what ways can intersectionality help you work alongside people from black and ethnic minority backgrounds with mental health challenges to help them engage with services?
- The dominant discourse of young black men with mental health problems is that they are dangerous and threatening. How might an intersectional lens help you to challenge this narrative?
- How might intersectionality be used in mental health social work to understand processes of marginalisation and exclusion influencing mental health?

References

Adkison-Bradley, Carla, Donna-Maria Maynard, Phillip Johnson, and Stephaney Carter. 2009. British African Caribbean women and depression. *British Journal of Guidance and Counselling* 37 (1): 65–72.

Alleyne, Aileen. 2005. Invisible injuries and silent witnesses: The shadow of racial oppression in workplace contexts. *Psychodynamic Practice* 11 (3): 283–299.

Anand, Aradhana S., and Raymond Cochrane. 2005. The mental health status of South Asian women in Britain: A review of the UK literature. *Psychology and Developing Societies* 17 (2): 195–214.

Ashley, Wendy. 2014. The angry black woman: The impact of pejorative stereotypes on psychotherapy with black women. *Social Work in Public Health* 29 (1): 27–34.

Barnett, Phoebe, Euan Mackay, Hannah Matthews, Rebecca Gate, Helen Greenwood, Kevin Ariyo, Kamaldeep Bhui, Kristoffer Halvorsrud, Stephen Pilling, and Shubulade Smith. 2019. Ethnic variations in compulsory detention under the mental health act: A systematic review and meta-analysis of international data. *The Lancet* 6 (4): 305–317.

Batsleer, Janet, Khatidja Chantler, and Erica Burman. 2003. Responses of health and social care staff to South Asian Women who attempt suicide and/or self-harm. *Journal of Social Work Practice* 17 (1): 103–114.

BASW. 2014. *The Code of Ethics for Social Work.* London: The Policy, Ethics and Human Rights Committee.

Bécares, Laila, James Nazroo, and Yvonne Kelly. 2015. A longitudinal examination of maternal, family, and area-level experiences of racism on children's socioemotional development: Patterns and possible explanations. *Social Science and Medicine* 142: 128–135.

Bécares, Laila, and James Nazroo. 2013. Social capital, ethnic density and mental health among ethnic minority people in England: a mixed-methods study. *Ethnicity and Health* 18 (6): 544–562.

Bhui, Kamaldeep, Kristoffer Halvorsrud, and James Nazroo. 2018. Making a difference: Ethnic inequality and severe mental illness. *The British Journal of Psychiatry* 213 (4): 574–578.

Bignall, Tracey, Samir Jeraj, Emily Helsby and Jabeer Butt. 2019. *Racial Disparities in Mental Health: Literature and Evidence Review.* London: Race Equality Foundation.

Bland, Robert, Noel Renouf, and Ann Tullgren. 2009. *Social Work Practice in Mental Health: An Introduction.* Crow's Nest, NSW: Allen and Unwin.

Borschmann, Rohan D., Steven Gillard, Kati Turner, Mary Chambers, and Aileen O'Brien. 2010. Section 136 of the Mental Health Act: A new literature review. *Medicine, Science and the Law* 50 (1): 34–39.

Bryant-Davis, Thema, and Carlota Ocampo. 2005. The trauma of racism. *The Counseling Psychologist* 33 (4): 574–578.

Bryant-Davis, Thema, and Carlota Ocampo. 2006. A therapeutic approach to the treatment of racist-incident-based trauma. *Journal of Emotional Abuse* 6 (4): 1–22.

Bryne, Bridget. Claire Alexander, Omar Khan, James Nazroo and William Shankley. 2020. *Ethnicity, Race and Inequality in the UK: State of the Nation.* Bristol: Policy Press.

Carr, Sarah. 2014. Critical perspectives on intersectionality. In *Rethinking Anti-Discriminatory and Anti-Oppressive Theories for Social Work Practice*, eds. Christine Cocker and Trish Hafford-Letchfield, 140–153. Basingstoke: Palgrave Macmillan.

Chakraborty, Apu, Kwame McKenzie, and Michael King. 2009. Discrimination, ethnicity and psychosis: A qualitative study. *Ethnicity and Inequalities in Health and Social Care* 2 (1): 18–29.

Chakraborty, Apu, Lance Patrick, and Maria Lambri. 2013. Racism and mental illness in the UK. In *Mental Disorders: Theoretical and Empirical Perspectives*, eds. Robert Woolfolk and Lesley Allen, 119–156. Rijeka, Croatia: InTech.

Chantler, Khatidja. 2003. South Asian women: Exploring systemic service inequalities around attempted suicide and self-harm. *European Journal of Social Work* 6 (1): 33–48.

Chantler, Khatidja. 2007. Border crossings: nationhood, gender, culture and violence. *International Journal of Critical Psychology* 20: 138–166.

Chantler, Khatidja. 2012. Recognition of and intervention in forced marriage as a form of violence and abuse. *Trauma, Violence, and Abuse* 13 (3): 176–183.

Chantler, Khatidja. 2012. Gender, asylum seekers and mental distress: Challenges for mental health social work. *British Journal of Social Work* 42 (2): 318–334.

Chantler, Khatidja, Geetanjali Gangoli, and Marianne Hester. 2009. Forced marriage in the UK: Religious, cultural, economic or state violence? *Critical Social Policy* 29 (4): 587–612.

Chantler, Khatidja, Geetanjali Gangoli, and Ravi K. Thiara. 2018. Muslim women and gender based violence in India and the UK. *Critical Social Policy* 39 (2): 163–183.

Chantler, Khatidja, and Melanie McCarry. 2019. Forced marriage, coercive control, and conducive contexts: The experiences of women in Scotland. *Violence Against Women* 26 (1): 89–109.

Comas-Díaz, Lillian. 2016. *Racial trauma recovery: A race-informed therapeutic approach to racial wounds.* In *The Cost of Racism for People of Color: Contextualizing Experiences of Discrimination,* eds. Alvin N. Alvarez, Christopher T. H. Liang, and Helen A. Neville, 249–272. Washington DC: American Psychological Association.

Cudjoe, Louisa, Sarah Barber, and Graham Thornicroft. 2019. Tackling inequalities: A partnership between mental health services and black faith communities. *Journal of Mental Health* 28 (3): 225–228.

Dein, Simon, and Abdool S. Illaiee. 2013. Jinn and mental health: Looking at jinn possession in modern psychiatric practice. *The Psychiatrist* 37 (9): 290–293.

Department of Health. 2011. *No Health Without Mental Health: A Cross-Government Mental Health Outcomes Strategy for People of All Ages.* London: Stationery Office.

Department of Health. 2019. Modernising the mental health act: Final report from the independent review. London: Stationery Office.

Edge, Dawn, Deborah Baker and Anne Rogers. 2004. Perinatal depression among black Caribbean women. *Health and Social Care in the Community* 12 (5): 430–438.

Fernando, Suman. 2010. *Mental Health, Race and Culture.* Basingstoke: Palgrave Macmillan.

Fernando, Suman. 2012. Race and culture issues in mental health and some thoughts on ethnic identity. *Counselling Psychology Quarterly* 25 (2): 113–123.

Fernando, Suman. 2017. *Institutional Racism in Psychiatry and Clinical Psychology: Race Matters in Mental Health.* Basingstoke: Palgrave Macmillan.

Fernando, Suman, and Frank Keating. 2009. *Mental Health in a Multi-Ethnic Society.* London: Routledge.

Fernando, Suman, and Roy Moodley. 2018. *Global Psychologies: Mental Health and the Global South.* Basingstoke: Palgrave Macmillan.

Ford, Tamsin, Panos Vostanis, Howard Meltzer, and Robert Goodman. 2007. Psychiatric disorder among British children looked after by local authorities: Comparison with children living in private households. *British Journal of Psychiatry* 190 (4): 319–325.

Gangoli, Geetanjali, and Khatidja Chantler. 2009. Protecting victims of forced marriage: Is age a protective factor? *Feminist Legal Studies* 17 (3): 267–288.

Gajwani, Ruchika, Helen Parsons, Max Birchwood, and Swaran P. Singh. 2016. Ethnicity and detention: Are black and minority ethnic (BME) groups disproportionately detained under the Mental Health Act 2007? *Social Psychiatry and Psychiatric Epidemiology* 51 (5): 703–711.

Gilburt, Helen. 2018. Transforming children and young people's mental health provision – our response. London: The Kings Fund.

Gilburt, Helen. 2021. Understanding clinical decision-making at the interface of the Mental Health Act (1983) and the Mental Capacity Act (2005). London: The Kings Fund.

Goodman, Anna, Vikram Patel, and David A. Leon. 2008. Child mental health differences amongst ethnic groups in Britain: A systematic review. *BMC Public Health* 8 (258): 1–11.

Graham, Mekada J. 2007. *Black Issues in Social Work and Social Care.* Bristol: Policy Press.

Grey, Tracy, Hári Sewell, Gillian Shapiro, and Fahmida Ashraf. 2013. Mental health inequalities facing UK minority ethnic populations. *Journal of Psychological Issues in Organizational Culture* 3 (S1): 146–157.

Gutman, Leslie M., Heather Joshi, Lorraine Khan, and Ingrid Schoon. 2015. Children of the new century: mental health findings from the millennium cohort study. London: Centre for Mental Health. Available at: http://cdn.basw.co.uk/upload/basw_120221-1.pdf. Accessed 2 July 2020.

Hickson, Ford, Calum Davey, David Reid, Peter Weatherburn, and Adam Bourne. 2017. Mental health inequalities among gay and bisexual men in England, Scotland and Wales: A large community-based cross-sectional survey. *Journal of Public Health* 39 (2): 266–273.

Hill Collins, Patricia. 2019. *Intersectionality as Critical Social Theory.* Durham: Duke University Press.

Karban, Kate. 2017. Developing a health inequalities approach for mental health social work. *British Journal of Social Work* 47 (3): 885–992.

Keating, Frank. 2007. African and African Caribbean men and mental health. *Better Health Briefing* Paper 5. Available at: www.raceequalityfoundation.org.uk. Accessed 2 July 2020.

Keating, Frank. 2016. Racialized communities, producing madness and dangerousness. *Intersectionalities* 5 (3) 173–185.

Keating, Frank. 2020. Black men's conversations about mental health through photos. *Qualitative Social Work.* DOI: 10.1177/ 1473325020922293.

Keating, Frank, and David Robertson. 2004. Fear, black people and mental illness: A vicious circle? *Health and Social Care in the Community, 12* (5): 439–447.

Keating, Frank, Stephen Joseph, Kris Southby, and Pamela Fisher. 2019. Socially-oriented approaches to recovery for African and Caribbean men. Project Report. NIHR School for Social Care Research.

Keating, Frank, and Stefan Brown. 2016. Multidisciplinary contexts: Insights from mental health. In *Social Work in a Diverse Society: Transformative Practice with Black and Minority Ethnic Individuals and Communities*, eds. Charlotte Williams and Mekada J. Graham, 145–159. Bristol: Policy Press.

Khan, Lorraine, Geena Saini, Alex Augustine, Kyle Palmer, Mark Johnson, and Rohan Donald. 2017. *Against the Odds: Evaluation of the Mind Birmingham Up My Street Programme.* London: Centre for Mental Health. Available at: www.centreformentalhealth.org. uk. Accessed 1 July 2020.

Kim, Helen G., Jessica Kuendig, Kriti Prasad, and Anne Sexter. 2020. Exposure to racism and other adverse childhood experiences among perinatal women with moderate to severe mental illness. *Community Mental Health Journal* 56 (5): 867–874.

Kysar-Moon, Ashleigh. 2020. Childhood adversity and internalizing problems: Evidence of a race mental health paradox. *Society and Mental Health* 10 (2): 136–152.

Lane, Pauline, Rachel Tribe, and Rosa Hui. 2011. Intersectionality and the mental health of elderly Chinese women living in the UK. *International Journal of Migration, Health and Social Care* 6 (4): 34–41.

Linton, Samara, and Rianna Walcott, eds. 2018. *The Colour of Madness: Exploring BAME Mental Health in the UK.* Edinburgh: Stirling Publishing.

Littlewood, Roland, and Simon Dien. 2013. The doctor's medicine and the ambiguity of amulets: Life and suffering among Bangladeshi psychiatric patients and their families in London: An interview study – 1. *Anthropology and Medicine* 20 (3): 244–263.

Matsuoka, Atsuko. K. 2015. Ethnic/racial minority older adults and recovery: Integrating stories of resilience and hope in social work. *British Journal of Social Work* 45 (Supp. 1): 135–152.

Maynard, Kairo. 2018. To be black. To be a woman. Can dramatherapy help black women to discover their true self despite racial and gender oppression? *Dramatherapy* 39 (1): 31–48.

McAuley, Collette, and Ciara Young. 2006. The mental health of looked after children: Challenges for CAMHS provision. *Journal of Social Work Practice* 20 (1): 91–103.

Mehrotra, Gita. 2010. Toward a continuum of intersectionality theorizing for feminist social work scholarship. *Affilia* 25 (4): 417–430.

Memon, Anjum, Katie Taylor, Lisa M. Mohebati, Josefin Sundin, Max Cooper, Thomas Scanlon, and Richard de Visser. 2016. Perceived barriers to accessing mental health services among black and minority ethnic (BME) communities: A qualitative study in Southeast England. *BMJ Open* 6 (11): e012337.

HM Government. 2005. *Mental Capacity Act 2005.* London: Stationery Office.

Mental Health Foundation. 2018. What new statistics show about children's mental health. Available at: www.mentalhealth.org.uk/blog/what-new-statistics-show-about-childrens-mental-health. Accessed 2 July 2020.

Mental Health Foundation. 2020. *Tackling Social Inequalities to Reduce Mental Health Problems: How Everyone Can Flourish Equally.* London: Mental Health Foundation.

Mhemooda, Malek, and Carol Joughin, eds. 2004. *Mental Health Services for Minority Ethnic Children and Adolescents.* London: Jessica Kingsley.

Miller, Catina, and Brigitte Vittrup. 2020. The indirect effects of police racial bias on African American families. *Journal of Family Issues* 41 (10): 1699–1722.

Moller, Naomi, Victoria Burgess, and Zainab Jogiyat. 2016. Barriers to counselling experienced by British South Asian women: A thematic analysis exploration. *Counselling and Psychotherapy Research* 16 (3): 201–210.

Morgan, Craig, Rosemarie Mallett, Gerard Hutchinson, and Julian Leff. 2004. Negative pathways to psychiatric care and ethnicity: The bridge between social science and psychiatry. *Social Science and Medicine* 58 (4): 739–752.

Newbigging, Karen, Mick McKeown, and Beverley French. 2013. Mental health advocacy and African and Caribbean men: Good practice principles and organizational models for delivery. *Health Expectations* 16 (1): 80–104.

NHS Digital. 2005. Mental health of children and young people in Great Britain. Available at: http://content.digital.nhs.uk/catalogue/PUB06116. Accessed 2 July 2020.

Pierce, Chester M. 1974. Psychiatric problems of the black minority. In *American Handbook of Psychiatry: Volume II: Child and Adolescent Psychiatry, Socio-Cultural and Community Psychiatry*, ed. Gerald Caplan, 512–523. New York: Basic Books.

Richardson, Joanna, and Carol Joughin. 2000. *The Mental Health Needs of Looked After Children.* London: The Royal College of Psychiatrists.

Robinson, Mark. Frank Keating, Steve Robertson 2013. Improving the mental health of BME men: Researching men's experiences. *Journal of Men's Health* 7 (3): 304–305.

Roe, Jenny. 2018. Ethnicity and children's mental health: Making the case for access to urban parks. *The Lancet* 2 (6): 234–235.

Sellers, Sherrill L., Earlise C. Ward, and David Pate. 2006. Dimensions of depression: A qualitative study of wellbeing among black African immigrant women. *Qualitative Social Work* 5 (1): 46–66.

Singh, Sarwan P., Nan Greenwood, Sarah White, and Rachel Churchill. 2007. Ethnicity and the mental health act 1983. *British Journal of Psychiatry* 191 (2): 99–105.

Smith, William A., Walter R. Allen, and Lynette L. Danley. 2007. 'Assume the position… You fit the description': Psychosocial experiences of racial battle fatigue among African American male college students. *American Behavioural Scientist* 51 (4): 551–578.

Synergi Collaborative Centre. 2018. The impact of racism on mental health. Available at: www.synergicollaborativecentre.co.uk. Accessed 6 December 2020.

Stanley, Nicky, Denise Riordan, and Helen Alaszewski. 2005. The mental health of looked after children: Matching response to need. *Health and Social Care in the Community* 13 (3): 239–248.

Sue, Derald W., Christina M. Capodilupo, Gina C.Torino, Jennifer M. Bucceri, Aisha M. B. Holder, Kevin L. Nadal, and Marta Esquilin. 2007. Racial microaggressions in everyday life. *American Psychologist* 62 (4): 271–286.

Tang, Lynn. 2017. *Recovery, Mental Health and Inequality: Chinese Ethnic Minorities as Mental Health Service Users*. London and New York: Routledge.

Tang, Lynn. 2019. Recovery, hope and agency: The meaning of hope amongst Chinese users of mental health services in the UK. *British Journal of Social Work* 49 (2): 282–299.

Walker, Sharon. 2020. Systemic racism: Big, black, mad and dangerous in the criminal justice system. In *The International Handbook of Black Community Mental Health*, eds. Richard Majors, Karen Carberry, and Theodore S. Ransaw, 41–60. Bingley: Emerald Publishing.

Wallace, Stephanie, James Nazroo, and Laia Bécares. 2016. Cumulative effect of racial discrimination on the mental health of ethnic minorities in the United Kingdom. *Public Health* 106 (7): 1294–1300.

Watson, Helen, Deborah Harrop, Elizabeth Walton, Andy Young, and Hora Soltani. 2019. A systematic review of ethnic minority women's experiences of perinatal mental health conditions and services in Europe. *PLoS ONE* 14 (1): e0210587.

Williams, Monnica T., Isha W. Metzger, Chris Leins, and Celenia DeLapp. 2018. Assessing racial trauma within a DSM–5 framework: The UConn racial/ethnic stress and trauma survey. *Practice Innovations* 3 (4): 242–260.

Wilson, Melba. 2001. Black women and mental health: Working towards inclusive mental health services. *Feminist Review* 68 (1): 34–51.

Wilson, Melba. Shahana Ramsden and Michael Clark. 2009. Delivering race equality in mental health in England: The importance of pathways. *International Review of Psychiatry*. 21 (5): 427–429.

5 Intersectionality and social work with older people

Introduction

In this chapter I consider how an intersectional approach can be used in adult social care services with older people, defined here as aged 65 years and over. Firstly, I provide a brief overview of some key issues that affect the lived experiences of older people, followed by an exploration of the relevance of intersectionality for social work practice, particularly focusing on those from marginalised communities. Then, drawing on case scenarios, I illustrate how intersectionality can be employed in interventions with older people and conclude by considering some key points of reflection for person-centred practice in adult social care using intersectional approaches.

Factors that shape older people's experiences

Practice interventions with vulnerable older people pose many challenges for social workers, not least providing the right kind of care for increasing numbers of people (Duffy 2017). Notably, the changing landscape of ageing and demographics in the UK is leading to more diverse populations of older adults with a broad range of cultures and ethnicities, resulting in a much more complex range of health and social care issues to respond to in adult social care services (Chaney 2011; Hughes and Burch 2019; Katbamma and Matthews 2007; Toukan 2019). To begin with, there are a range of issues arising for older adults that result from socio-economic and health disparities. For example, research has highlighted age-related health problems such as osteoarthritis, dementia, heart disease, diabetes, depression, and impaired mobility (Hamilton-West et al. 2020; Hafford-Letchfield 2014; Phillipson and Ray 2016; Truswell 2020).

DOI: 10.4324/9780429467288-5

Furthermore, research into end-of-life care, work with vulnerable adults who may lack mental capacity, and complex safeguarding issues concerning adults who self-neglect identify a particular set of challenges for interventions with older people (Care Quality Commission 2016); Keating 2017; Milne 2009; Milne et al. 2014; Manthorpe and Martineau 2017; Preston-Shoot 2017). At the same time, there has been an increased recognition of the impact of social isolation and loneliness, which have a particularly pronounced effect on the health and well-being of older people (Courtin and Knapp 2017; Jovicic and McPherson 2020; Victor et al. 2012; Woodhead et al. 2004).

Moreover, it is important to understand the particular issues arising for older people from black and ethnic minority communities. Research suggests they are multiply disadvantaged by exposure to structural inequalities across the lifespan that create obstacles for a healthy old age (Bailey et al. 2018; Burholt et al. 2018; Centre for Policy on Ageing 2013; Care Quality Commission 2016; Milne 2020; Rajan-Rankin 2018; Torres 2019). An important consideration is that the problems facing older people from black and minority ethnic communities are intensified because in addition to exposure to race-related stressors, they are more likely to experience poverty-related difficulties that amplify the adversities in their lives and have a profoundly negative effect on their emotional, psychological, and physical health (Hayanga et al. 2020; Rajan-Rankin 2018). Therefore, the compounding effects of racism and ageism are further exacerbated for black and ethnic minority older people who face attitudinal and practical barriers in accessing support for social care needs (Khan 2017). Here, I borrow Crockett et al.'s (2016) concept of intersectional stigma, which they use to draw attention to the attitudinal, material and policy-driven obstacles that contribute to the vulnerability of older women from minority backgrounds.

As Humphries et al. (2016) and Lymbery (2019) explain, access to care depends increasingly on what people can afford and where they live, rather than on what they need. Social workers therefore have to make difficult decisions about eligibility for services, often with very limited resources. Certainly, major shifts in policy and practice have been prompted by the introduction of the Care Act 2014

(Penhale et al. 2017). In particular, the Care Act 2014 sets out the legal and policy framework for how local authorities should intervene with vulnerable adults in need of support (Cooper and Bruin 2017; Stanley 2016). More specifically, the Care Act 2014 has created new demands and expectations on local authorities in terms of their statutory duties around care planning and mental capacity assessments (Humphries et al. 2016). The point is made that the Care Act 2014 puts the principle of individual well-being and professional practice of the specific social worker at the centre of adult social care. Thus, practitioners need to apply a wide range of knowledge and skills to understand and manage diverse needs and complex risks. Significantly, the Care Act emphasises the importance of understanding and developing relationships with older people and their carers to enable and empower them to achieve best outcomes (Department of Health 2015).

What is the relevance of intersectionality for social work practice with older people?

Regarding the relevance of intersectionality for social work practice with older people, as noted elsewhere, intersectionality has come to be recognised as an influential feminist approach for making sense of how multiple oppressions manifest for older people, to develop emphatic and relational practice (Krekula 2007; McCormik 2008). Broadly, a feminist social work lens helps us to find ways of capturing how older women experience ageism in particularly gendered and racialised ways (Krekula 2007; Rajan-Rankin 2018; Ross-Sheriff 2008). The importance of an intersectional perspective for understanding the challenges of ageing in the contexts of racism, sexism, ableism, heterosexism, and classism has been underlined by a number of scholars (Cronin and King 2010; Fredriksen-Golden et al. 2019; Howard et al. 2019; Phillipson 2015). Importantly, when age is viewed through these lenses, it forces us to ask hard questions about how intersecting oppressions impact older people. Although it may seem obvious, there has to be a recognition that whether an adult with mental health issues, an older person, or an adult with dis-abilities, all inhabit multiple and overlapping identities such as age, gender, class, race, disability, and sexuality. In this regard, intersec-tionality may help us to think critically about how older people's expe-riences are impacted in significant and unique ways by these identity categories. Put differently, an intersectional perspective therefore helps us to engage with interlocking forms of oppression, rather than privileging one oppression over another. In other words, interrogat-ing ageing issues in social work from an intersectional perspective can help us to tease out the issues of multiple disadvantages, thus enabling a more critical grasp of the particular dynamics at play for ethnically diverse older persons, as well as the practical challenges for the policy and organisational context of practice in adult social care. Simply stated, looking at age discrimination through an inter-sectional lens offers us opportunities to dive deep into the issues unique to older people from diverse ethnic backgrounds. In this respect, an intersectional-informed approach challenges us to centre the experiences of adults with marginalised and stigmatised identi-ties whose experiences are rooted in oppression and discrimination. That is, when we engage intersectional thinking in social work with older people, it widens our scope for a more nuanced understanding of how interlocking oppressions manifest in everyday experiences for older people who need the support of adult social care services. The importance of intersectionality cannot be overstated for bringing into view the structural causes of the problems and issues that arise for older people to situate assessments within their lived realities.

In sum, it is likely that some social workers may struggle to see the relevance of intersectionality to their own day-to-day practice with older people. Nevertheless, it is also important to stress that an intersectionality lens aligns very closely with the core values of social work, as both are engaged with issues of social justice and anti-oppressive principles (International Federation of Social Work-ers 2014). As Hill Collins (2017) noted, social workers can engage intersectionality to inform their problem-solving strategies. What is perhaps most interesting is the particular role that intersectionality can play to enable professional curiosity, that is, the capability and skills needed to learn about and understand what is going on in an individual's life (Thacker et al. 2019). It is precisely because intersectionality offers a different way of conceptualising how subtle forms of oppressions are experienced that it is vital for working with diverse groups of older people for strengths-based interventions. In effect, an intersectionality perspective has the potential for interrogating the complexities to better understand the life experiences of older people using adult social care services.

With these points in mind, in the rest of the chapter I employ intersectionality to a case scenario to illustrate how race intersects with disability and ageism.

Having outlined some key issues of intersectionality and older adults, what follows are some practical approaches to apply intersectionality.

Case study

Family composition:

Maria: 84 years old
Shirley: 54 years old
Tom: 52 years old
Sharon: 19 years old
Fred: 15 years old

Maria is an 84-year-old black woman from Brazil, living in London for the last 20 years, who has recently been diagnosed with early-stage dementia. Maria's first language is Portuguese and, as she speaks very little English, she mainly socialises with the Portuguese speaking community. For the last six months, she has been living with her daughter Shirley's family.

Maria has become forgetful and regularly does not attend to her personal care. She is able to make a cup of tea, but cannot cook a meal or make a sandwich, due to being unable to sequence the events. Maria has good mobility and will often go out, leaving the front door open, sometimes dressed inappropriately, and gets confused once outside of the house. She will often attempt to speak with strangers. On two occasions, she has been brought home by neighbours who recognised her. She does not attend a day centre.

Maria has two sons, and a daughter, Shirley, who she lives with. One of her sons live outside of London in Kent, and the other lives in the neighbouring borough. They are both married with children and jobs. Shirley has requested support from her siblings in regard to the care of their mother, but this has been sporadic. Shirley describes that she feels very tired with caring for her mother, working full time, caring for her own family. Maria has recently had an official diagnosis at the local memory clinic of dementia.

Recently, Maria was found by a stranger walking in the rain, with a light jacket, no umbrella or handbag, and looking confused, when attempting to cross the main road. She was unable to say where she was going. The person who found her called the police, who looked through her pocket and found Shirley's phone number on a piece of paper. Police were given the address and brought Maria home. Shirley was tearful and explained to the police that she is having difficulties caring for her mother. The police officer advised her to contact social services, and they also completed a safeguarding adult referral, which was sent to social services. The social worker on duty contacted the family to arrange a home visit; when she arrived at the family home, she learned that Maria does not speak English.

It is safe to say that the intersections of race, age, gender, and migration background mean Maria is positioned as a multiply marginalised older black woman with a disability that is not yet apparent. It is useful, then, to consider how the practical application of an intersectional approach might inform the assessment and intervention with Maria and her family.

Let us consider that Maria has a neurological condition that impairs cognitive functioning that will affect changes in emotions, perception, and behaviour (DeWaal 2014). In the main, dementia is a progressive condition that typically has an impact on a range of things including: memory, orientation, ability to think, language, and decision-making (World Health Organization 2019). In a practical sense, the loss of autonomy, choice, and control that comes with dementia will be a core challenge for Maria (De Waal 2014). Keeping this in mind, in terms of quality of life and well-being, dementia will profoundly affect not only how Maria thinks and feels, but will also decrease her ability to complete tasks and make decisions that enable her to live safely and independently (Innes 2009; Manthorpe 2004). Intersectionality therefore offers a framework for looking at discrimination, marginalisation, and the rights of people with dementia (Edvardsson and Innes 2010; Innes and Manthorpe 2012; Innes et al. 2021). Intersectionality is well-positioned to elicit a better understanding of the concerns that Maria's dementia diagnosis presents to her and her family. Moreover, it can be argued that such an approach provokes thinking about the core elements of Maria's intersectional experiences. Its strengths thus lie in being able to take a closer look at the factors that frame the issues that she and her family will have to confront to get the best health and well-being results. In its own way, intersectionality therefore directs us to think critically about how to effectively intervene to support Maria and her family.

In situations like Maria's, using the lens of intersectionality helps us to think critically about dementia in the context of her racialised gendered identity. From this perspective, the particularities of the issues that Maria will have to navigate can be better understood. A key point is that, in order to promote choice and control for Maria to feel supported and empowered, the appropriate sources of support will need to be provided.

There is little doubt that the dynamics of dementia communication will present Maria with a range of challenges (Wray 2020). Maria is currently diagnosed with early-stage dementia and one challenging aspect is that she is experiencing attentional deficit and memory impairment. This, in itself, makes things difficult, because her capacity to advocate for herself will diminish; the Mental Capacity Act (2005), which sets out the guidelines to follow if someone with cognitive impairments cannot make decisions for themselves, can be drawn upon to help make decisions in Maria's best interests. Moreover, it is fair to say that Maria has some additional needs with regards to language and communication which would act as a barrier to her accessing services. One option is for an application to be made for direct payments, as opposed to the local authority putting a package of care in place, enabling a more personalised package of care that is particularly useful for service users whose first language is not English, as they can often source mother tongue carers from their own networks. It is important for social workers to be thinking outside of the box, as opposed to a reliance on traditional packages of care options, such as day centres.

These matters are of central importance for appreciating the obstacles that Maria will encounter in communicating her needs and wants to carers; there is also a danger that she may not be asked directly for her views about her care package, therefore her needs might be overlooked. Part of the problem is that, because language and communication are negatively affected by dementia, it is often assumed that those with dementia will not be lucid enough to be able to communicate their wishes and feelings (Innes et al. 2021; Wray 2020). An intersectional lens can help us to attend to the additional barriers that might result in Maria's further marginalisation and isolation. What is most important about an intersectional approach is that it provides a framework with which to conceptualise Maria's dementia at the centre of her experiences.

Applying a framework of intersectionality to dementia care offers a critical lens to capture the multi-faceted ways Maria's identity overlaps in experiences of dementia. The interaction of race, ability, age, and gender is central to recognising and understanding how these categories overlap to shape Maria's experiences of dementia in complex ways (Hulko et al. 2020). Given Maria's social location and identity as a black, older woman, such elements will have significant bearing on her day-to-day realities with dementia. It is therefore useful to pay particular attention to the ways that race interacts with disability, age, and gender to recognise the cultural and identity issues impacting Maria's lived experience of dementia. Employing an intersectional approach to dementia allows us to ask important questions about the multiplicity of Maria's identity. Thus, utilising an intersectional frame helps us to understand Maria's raced experiences of dementia at the intersection of gender and age.

How, for example, might she be referred to; as an older woman, an older woman with a disability, an older woman who is black, with dementia? If Maria is seen only as an older person with dementia, then there would be a disregard for how her race, gender, and socio-economic background intersect with age, which would fail to capture the nuances of her care needs (Chapple et al. 2021; Holman and Walker 2020). To this end, understanding Maria's diagnosis of dementia through an intersectional lens encourages a shift in emphasis from a medical model of dementia care to a social model approach (Keating 2017). Specifically, incorporating insights from intersectionality directs attention to how dementia further compounds Maria's experience of ageing. An appreciation of these factors will enable us to be cognisant of how Maria's multiple identities interact to better understand how she can be supported in a culturally sensitive way.

While it is important that the overriding concern has to be about Maria's care needs, attention must also be given to her family's support needs as family caregivers are a vital source of dementia care (Johl et al. 2016; Manthorpe 2004). Indeed, Maria's diagnosis of dementia will be worrying for her family and will significantly impact family relationships (Truswell 2020; Wray 2020). With regards to post-diagnosis support, Maria's family will need to have the basics of dementia explained to them, especially how it affects the social, emotional, and relational aspects of Maria's life, to enable a good understanding of her care needs (Truswell 2020). They will also need to understand the progression stages of dementia and how they will affect her long-term care. It bears pointing out that at different stages of dementia (mild, moderate, or severe), Maria's symptoms will change, and she may not be able to engage in emotional self-regulation. Intersectionality is therefore ideal, as it can help surface the myriad ways Maria and her family's cultural values and beliefs could affect the ways her needs might be interpreted and responded to. Also problematic is that deep-rooted cultural values and expectations about family responsibilities to provide kinship care for vulnerable members might be a barrier for family caregivers in asking for help and support from adult social care services (Truswell 2020; Johl et al. 2016). For instance, Maria's family may feel an obligation to care for her, and especially Shirley, who is currently providing the greater part of the care, may need support to express any uncomfortable feelings such as guilt, ambivalence, denial, and other issues that may arise for her. The family's strengths and vulnerabilities will need to be explored in a sensitive way to deepen an understanding of the day-to-day realities of living with someone with dementia (Johl et al. 2016). It will be important to discern whether Shirley may have concerns that the mental and emotional load of caring for Maria will fall solely on her without any practical support from adult social care (Milne and Chryssanthopoulou 2005; Innes 2021). Crucially important, intersectionality therefore opens up opportunities to engage with the concerns that Shirley has raised about the difficulty of balancing her paid work, caring for her children, and her caregiving role with regards to Maria. Typically, the disproportionate burden of unpaid care work falls heavily on women (Ophir and Polos 2021). That is to say, intersectional thinking can help elucidate the gendered dimensions of unpaid care responsibilities. Essentially, intersectionality can enable a more nuanced assessment of the issues that Shirley has to wrestle with to better understand what forms of support she might need in her caregiving role.

Because intersectionality offers a way for a more nuanced discussion of the interplay of contextual factors that impact, it therefore helps us to better understand Maria's lived experience of dementia for building strengths-based interventions that are responsive to her needs. More generally, intersectionality is a useful tool for fostering an anti-oppressive approach to provide practice that is rooted in principles of person-centred care, self-hood and relationship-based social work (Dilworth-Anderson et al. 2020; Kitwood 1997). In other words, intersectionality provides space for reflection in social work to actively engage with service users with multiple categories of identities. For this reason, intersectionality equips social workers with the conceptual tools that they need for navigating the complexity of factors for vulnerable older adults with dementia like Maria.

Conclusion

In this chapter, I have sketched some of the ways in which an inter-sectionality theoretical lens can be used to respond to the needs of older adults living at the intersection of multiple marginalised identities. Specifically, I have illuminated that the ageing experiences of black and ethnic minority older adults are multi-faceted because they face differ-ent barriers as a result of various intersecting inequalities. With the use of a case study, I illustrated some ways in which intersectionality can be applied practically to engage with the intersecting inequalities impacting black and ethnic minority older adults who access support from adult social care services. Arguably, the adoption of an intersectional lens draws attention to how interlocking forms of oppression exacerbate the later life concerns of older adults. Importantly, applying intersectionality can cultivate a critical lens through which ageism and its interrelated-ness with other identity categories can be interpreted to deepen con-versations about the lived experiences of older adults from black and ethnic minority backgrounds. To be clear, the application of intersection-ality affords a greater recognition and appreciation of how life course experiences, health inequalities and structural factors affect the later life care and support needs of older adults who have to traverse multiple intersecting factors. To this end, intersectionality can stimulate profes-sional curiosity to understand the challenges facing older adults from black and ethnic minority communities in need of services and support. More importantly, because intersectionality eschews homogenising older adults, it forces social workers to engage in critical conversations to identify considerations for innovative approaches for interventions that can capture the heterogeneity within diverse groups of older adults.

Key points

- Intersectionality has great relevance for understanding how age, race, gender, sexuality, disability, and class intersect with each other to frame the psychosocial needs of older adults who require social care services.

- In social work, the need to view older adults' identities from an intersectional approach is critical for understanding their relationships, and the social and cultural factors influencing their lived experiences.
- Intersectionality offers a uniquely critical lens to make sense of the structural disadvantage that lies at the heart of aged care needs of older adults from black and ethnic minority backgrounds.

Reflective questions

- In which ways can intersectionality be used to reflect on practice for the care and support needs of older adults from black and ethnic minority backgrounds?
- How might intersectional approaches be used to develop critical reflection skills for supporting older adults from black and ethnic minority groups to navigate social care services?
- How might applying intersectionality help to understand the processes and policy decisions that frame assessments about need with black and ethnic minority older adults?
- How might social workers use intersectionality to help older adults identify their own outcomes and give meaning to their lived experiences and engage with support?

References

Bailey, Cathy, Zeibeda Sattar, and Parveen Akhtar. 2018. Older South Asian Women sharing their perceptions of health and social care services and support: A participatory inquiry. *Wiley Health Science Reports* 1 (8): https://onlinelibrary.wiley.com/doi/full/10.1002/hsr2.55.

Bauer, Greta R., and Ayden I. Scheim. 2019. Methods for analytic intercategorical intersectionality in quantitative research: Discrimination as a mediator of health inequalities. *Social Science and Medicine* 226: 236–245.

Boyle, Geraldine. 2014. Recognising the agency of people with dementia. *Disability and Society* 29 (7): 1130–1144.

Burholt, Vanessa, Christine Dobbs, and Christina Victor. 2018. Social support networks of older migrants in England and Wales: The role of collectivist culture. *Ageing and Society* 38 (7): 1453–1477.

Care Quality Commission. 2016. A different ending: addressing inequalities in end of life care. *Care Quality Commission*: 20160505 CQC_EOLC_GoodPractice_FINAL_2.

Centre for Policy on Ageing. 2013. *The ageing of ethnic minority population of England and Wales: Findings from the 2011 Census.* Available at: www.cpa.org.uk/information/reviews/theageingofthe-ethnicminoritypopulationsofenglandandwales-findingsfromthe-2011census.pdf. Accessed 23 January 2021.

Chaney, Paul. 2011. Mainstreaming intersectional equality for older people? Exploring the impact of quasi-federalism in the UK. *Public Policy Administration* 28 (1): 21–42.

Chapple, Reshawna L., Binnae A. Bridwell, and Kishonna L. Gray. 2021. Exploring intersectional identity in black deaf women: The complexity of the lived experience in college. *Affilia*: https://journals.sagepub.com/doi/10.1177/0886109920985769.

Cooper, Adi, and Claire Bruin. 2017. Adult safeguarding and the Care Act (2014): The impacts on partnerships and practice. *Journal of Adult Protection* 19 (4): 209–219.

Crockett, Cailin, Bergen Cooper, and Bonnie Brandi. 2018. Intersectional stigma and late-life intimate-partner and sexual violence: How social workers can bolster safety and healing for older survivors. *British Journal of Social Work* 48 (4): 1000–1013.

Cronin, Ann, and Andrew King. 2010. Power, inequality and identification: Exploring diversity and intersectionality amongst older LGB adults. *Sociology* 44 (5): 876–892.

Courtin, Emilie, and Martin Knapp. 2017. Social isolation, loneliness and health in old age: A scoping review. *Health and Social Care in the Community* 25 (3): 799–812.

Department of Health. 2015. Knowledge and skills statement for social workers in adult services: basw_115420-2_0.

De Waal, Hugo. 2014. Rethinking dementia: How autonomy and control can be fostered through the development of person-centred services. *Working with Older People* 18 (2): 82–89.

Dilworth-Anderson, Peggy, Heehyul Moon, and María P. Aranda. 2020. Dementia caregiving research: Expanding and reframing the lens of diversity, inclusivity, and intersectionality. *The Gerontologist* 60 (5): 797–805.

Duffy, Francis. 2017. A social work perspective on how ageist language, discourses and understandings negatively frame older people and why taking a critical social work stance is essential. *British Journal of Social Work* 47 (7): 2068–2085.

Edvardsson, David. and Innes, Anthia. 2010. Measuring person-centred care: A critical comparative review of published tools. *The Gerontologist* 50 (6): 834–846.

Fredriksen Goldsen, Karen, Sarah Jen, and Anna Muraco. 2019. Iridescent life course: LGBTQ ageing research and blueprint for the future: A systematic review. *Gerontology* 65 (3): 253–274.

Hafford-Letchfield, Trish. 2014. Critical educational gerontology: What has it got to offer social work with older people? *European Journal of Social Work* 17 (3): 443–446.

Hamilton-West, Kate, Alisoun Milne, and Sarah Hotham. 2020. New horizons in supporting older people's health and wellbeing: Is social prescribing a way forward? *Age and Ageing* 49 (3): 319–326.

Hayanga, Brenda, Dylan Kneale, and Ann Phoenix. 2020. Understanding the friendship networks of older black and minority ethnic people living in the United Kingdom. *Ageing and Society* 1–20: doi:10.1017/S0144686X19001624.

Hill Collins, Patricia. 2017. The difference that power makes: Intersectionality and participatory democracy. *Investigaciones Feministas* 8 (1): 19–39.

Holman, Daniel, and Alan Walker. 2020. Understanding unequal ageing: Towards a synthesis of intersectionality and life course analyses. *European Journal of Ageing*. https://doi.org/10.1007/s10433-020-00582-7.

Howard, Susanna, Kevin L. Lee, Aviva G. Nathan, Hannah C. Wenger, Marshall H. Chin, Scott C. Cook. 2019. Healthcare experiences of transgender people of color. *Journal of General Internal Medicine* 34 (1): 2068–2074.

Hughes, Susanne, and Sarah Burch. 2019. 'I'm not just a number on a sheet, I'm a person': Domiciliary care, self and getting older. *Health and Social Care in the Community* 28 (3): 903–912.

Hulko, Wendy, Shari Brotman, Louise Stern, and Ilyan Ferrer. 2020. *Gerontological Social Work in Action: Anti-oppressive Practice with Older Adults, Their Families, and Communities*. London: Routledge.

Humphries, Richard, Ruth Thorlby, Holly Holder, Patrick Hall and Anna Charles. 2016. *Social Care for Older People: Home Truths*. London: The King's Fund. Available at: www.kingsfund.org.uk/publications/social-care-older-people. Accessed 2 October 2020.

Innes, Anthea. 2009. *Dementia Studies: A Social Science Perspective*. London: Sage.

Innes, Anthea and Jill Manthorpe. 2012. Developing theoretical understandings of dementia and their application to dementia care policy in the UK. *Dementia* 12 (6): 682–696.

Innes, Anthea, Lesley Calvert, and Gail Bowker. 2021. *Dementia: The Basics*. London: Routledge.

International Federation of Social Workers. 2014. Global agenda for social work and social development 2014: First report. *International Social Work* 57 (Supp 4): 3–16.

Johl, Nicholas, Tom Patterson, and Lesley Pearson. 2016. What do we know about the attitudes, experiences and needs of black and minority ethnic carers of people with dementia in the United Kingdom? A systematic review of empirical research findings. *Dementia* 15 (4): 721–742.

Jovicic, Ana, and Susan McPherson. 2020. To support and not to cure: A general practitioner management of loneliness. *Health and Social Care in the Community* 28 (2): 376–384.

Katbamma, Savita, and Ruth Matthews. 2007. *Ageing and Ethnicity in England: A Demographic Profile of BME Older People in England*. London: Age Concern England.

Keating, Frank. 2017. Dementia: Challenges for social work education in Europe. *European Journal of Social Work* 20 (3): 422–428.

Khan, Omar. 2017. Race is no protection against loneliness. In *Alone in the Crowd: Loneliness and Diversity*, eds. Kate Joplin and Andrew Barnett. Available at: www.ageingwellinwales.com/Libraries/Documents/Alone-in-the-Crowd---Loneliness-and-Diversity.pdf. Accessed 23 January 2021.

Kitwood, Tom. 1997. *Dementia Reconsidered: The Person Comes First*. Buckingham: Open University Press.

Krekula, Clary. 2007. The intersection of age and gender: Reworking gender theory and social gerontology. *Current Sociology* 55 (2): 155–171.

Lui, Xiayang. Glenda Cook. and Mimma Cattan. 2017. Support networks for Chinese older immigrants accessing English health and social care services: The concept of bridge people. *Health and Social Care in the Community* 25 (2), 667–677.

Lymbery, Michael. 2019. The slow death of social work with older people? In *What is the Future of Social Work? A Handbook for Positive Action*, ed. Michael Lavalette, 39–57. Bristol: Policy Press.

Manthorpe, Jill. 2004. Risk taking. In *Dementia and Social Inclusion: Marginalised Groups and Marginalised Areas of Dementia Research, Care and Practice*, eds. Anthea Innes, Carole Archibald, and Charlie Murphy, 137–153. London: Jessica Kingsley.

Manthorpe, Jill, Jo Moriarty, Martin Stevens, Nadira Sharif, Shereen Hussein. 2010. *Supporting Black and Minority Ethnic Older People's Mental Wellbeing: Accounts of Social Care Practice*. London: Social Care Institute for Excellence.

Manthorpe Jill, and Alison Bowes. 2010. Age ethnicity and equalities: Policy and practice messages from recent studies of elder abuse in the UK. *Social Policy and Society* 9 (2): 255–26.

Manthorpe, Jill and Stephen Martineau. 2017. Pressure Points: learning from Serious Case Reviews of failures of care and pressure ulcer problems in care homes. *The Journal of Adult Protection* 19 (5): 284–296.

Marmot, Michael, Jessica Allen, Tammy Boyce, Peter Goldblatt, and Joana Morrison. 2020. Health equity in England: The Marmot Review 10 years on. *British Medical Journal* 368: m693.

McCormik, Marie L. 2008. Women's bodies aging culture, context, and social work practice. *Affilia* 23 (4): 312–323.

Milne, Alisoun. 2009. Mental health and well-being in later life, defini-
   tions and determinants and addressing the challenges to mental
   health and well-being in later life. In *Older People's Mental Health
   Today: A Handbook*, ed. Toby Williamson. Shoreham-by-Sea:
   Pavilion Publishing.

Milne, Alisoun. 2020. *Mental Health in Later Life.* Bristol: Policy Press.

Milne, Alisoun, and Christina Chryssanthopoulou. 2005. Dementia
   care-giving in Black and Asian populations: Reviewing and refin-
   ing the research agenda. *Journal of Community & Applied Social
   Psychology* 15 (5): 319–337.

Milne, Alisoun, Mary Pat Sullivan, Denise Tanner, Sally Richards, Mo
   Ray, Liz Lloyd, Christian Beech, and Judith Philips. 2014. *Social
   Work with Older People: A Vision for the* Future. London: The
   College of Social Work. www.scie-socialcareonline.org.uk/social-
   work-with-older-people-a-vision-for-the   future/r/a11G0000003jh-
   5FIAQ. Accessed 25 September 2018.

Mental Health Foundation. 2015. *Dementia, Rights, and the Social
   Model of Disability: A New Direction for Policy and Practice*? London: Mental Health Foundation.

Ophir, Ariane and Jessica Polos. 2021. Care life expectancy: Gender
   and unpaid work in the context of population aging. *Population
   Research and Policy Review*. https://doi.org/10.1007/s11113-021-
   09640-z.

Parveen, Sahdia, Carol Peltier, and Jan R. Oyebode. 2017. Perceptions of dementia and use of services in minority ethnic communities: A scoping exercise. *Health and Social Care in the Community*
   25 (2): 734–742.

Penhale, Bridget, Alison Brammer, Pete Morgan, Paul Kingston, and
   Michael Preston-Shoot. 2017. The Care Act 2014: A new legal
   framework for safeguarding adults in civil society. *Journal of Adult
   Protection* 19 (4): 169–174.

Phillipson, Chris. 2015. Placing ethnicity at the center of studies of
   later life: Theoretical perspectives and empirical challenges. *Ageing and Society* 35 (5): 917–934.

Phillipson, Chris, and Mo Ray. 2016. Ageing in urban environments:
   Challenges and opportunities for a critical social work practice. In

Social Work and The City: Urban Themes in 21st Century Social Work, ed. Charlotte Williams, 151–172. London: Palgrave Macmillan.

Preston-Shoot, Michael. 2017. On self-neglect and safeguarding adult reviews: Diminishing returns or adding value? *The Journal of Adult Protection* 19 (2): 53–66.

Proctor, Gillian. 2001. Listening to older women with dementia. *Disability and Society* 16 (3): 361–376.

Ophir, Ariane, and Jessica Polos. 2021. Care life expectancy: Gender and unpaid work in the context of population aging. *Population Research and Policy Review*: https://doi.org/10.1007/s11113-021-09640-z.

Rajan-Rankin, Sweta. 2018. Race, embodiment and later life: Re-animating aging bodies of color. *Journal of Aging Studies* 45: 32–38.

Ross-Sheriff, Fariyal. 2008. Aging and gender, feminist theory and social work practice concerns. *Affilia* 23 (4): 309–311.

Runnymede Trust. 2020. Researching older black and minority ethnic people and financial inclusion. London: Runnymede Trust.

Stanley, Tony. 2016. A practice framework to support the Care Act 2014. *The Journal of Adult Protection* 18 (1): 53–64.

Thacker, Helen, Ann Anka, and Bridget Penhale. 2019. Could curiosity save lives? An exploration into the value of employing professional curiosity and partnership work in safeguarding adults under the Care Act 2014. *Journal of Adult Protection* 21 (5): 252–267.

Torres, Sandra. 2019. Ethnicity, race and care in older age: what can a social justice framework offer? In *Ageing, Diversity and Equality: Social Justice Perspectives*, ed. Sue Westwood, 167–180. London: Routledge.

Toukan, Zein. 2019. The aging population. *InnovAiT* 12 (5): 239–242.

Truswell, David. 2020. Introduction. In *Supporting People Living with Dementia in Black, Asian and Minority Ethnic Communities*, ed. David Truswell, 15–20. London: Jessica Kingsley.

Victor, Christina R., Vanessa Burholt, and Wendy Martin. 2012. Loneliness and ethnic minority elders in Great Britain: An exploratory study. *Journal of Cross-cultural Gerontology* 27 (1): 65–78.

Woodhead, Gillian, Michael Calnan, Paul Dieppe, and Win Tadd. 2004. Dignity in older age: What do older people in the United Kingdom think? *Age and Ageing* 33 (2): 165–170.

World Health Organization. 2019. Dementia. Available at: www.who.int/newsroom/fact-sheets/detail/dementia. Accessed 23 January 2021.

Wray, Alison. 2020. *The Dynamics of Dementia Communication.* New York: Oxford University Press.

6 Intersectionality as pedagogical practice in social work education

In this chapter, I shift attention to address how intersectionality can be used as a pedagogical practice in social work education. Here I focus on how intersectionality as an analytical lens can be used by social work educators to interrogate intersecting and overlapping systems of oppression. Placing emphasis on issues of power, oppression, and social inequalities, I consider intersectionality as a pedagogical practice to show what intersectional approaches can offer social work education for the teaching of a range of topics for practice with diverse populations. To these ends, I will employ two examples of intersectional pedagogical tools to illustrate how intersectionality can be integrated in social work education.

Intersectional pedagogy

From the 1970s onwards, anti-oppressive scholars have advocated for educators to embed analyses of social inequalities, oppression and social justice in social work education and practice (Ahmad 1990; Aymer 2002; Bhatti-Sinclair 2011; Dominelli 1988; Graham and Schiele 2010; Hicks 2008; Keating 2000; Smethurst and Bhatti-Sinclair 2017; Dunk-West and Hafford-Letchfield 2011; Williams 2016), setting the stage for engaging with debates of social identities and experiences for pedagogy and praxis, and producing a rich body of knowledge to advance the social justice agenda in social work. Specifically, a number of intersectional social work scholars (for example, Busche et al. 2012; Joy 2019; Mattsson 2013; Mehrotra 2010; Murphy et al. 2009; Robinson et al. 2016), remind us of the importance of intersectionality as a tool to assist with addressing lived experiences that result from multiply marginalised and oppressed identities. As noted by Robinson et al. (2016), because

DOI: 10.4324/9780429467288-6

intersectionality's goals are justice-oriented, it therefore provides a critical set of tools for understanding multiple categories of subtle and overt forms of power and oppression that pervade much social work. Intersectionality helps elucidate what Mattson (2014) in her pivotal article, 'Intersectionality as a useful tool: Anti-oppressive social work and critical reflection', describes as the potential of traditional social work to reinforce oppression and inequality.

As indicated in Chapter 2, the core concepts of intersectionality, namely social inequality, relationality, power, social context, complexity, and social justice, chime very well with social work values. Intersectionality thus provides some analytic tools to advance a social justice perspective for social work. The intersectionality wheel (Simpson 2009) is an important resource for using with learners to develop their understandings of what Murphy et al. (2009,) refer to as the person-in-environment.

The intersectionality wheel is an analytical device that can help learners engage with discourses of oppression and discrimination to prepare for practice with diverse individuals and groups (Simpson 2009). Specifically, Simpson identifies four distinctive domains in the intersectional wheel. The first domain depicts a person's distinctive circumstances, the second signifies important dimensions that shape an individual's social identity, the third represents the multiple forms of oppression that effect identity, and the fourth characterises the structural, institutional, and societal factors that work together to reinforce systems of oppression. The intersectional wheel thus illustrates the ways that intersecting axes of oppression and their interrelatedness present unique challenges for subordinated individuals, groups, and communities (Murphy et al. 2009). This conceptual model can therefore be utilised to help students unpack the interactions of myriad factors that have an influence for individuals, to open up conversations about working across difference for understanding the heterogeneity of experience.

In teaching about anti-oppressive practice, the challenge is always how to engage students who often struggle to recognise and articulate their personal value orientation and beliefs, to understand what such factors mean for addressing their own positionalities (Philips and

Cree 2014). The intersectionality wheel can be a catalyst for students to lay the groundwork for understanding their own location within the privilege-oppression spectrum (Abrams and Molo 2009). Used as a reflection tool, the intersectionality wheel can provide a framework for understanding and theorising multiple forms of oppression experienced by marginalised groups (Bernard 2019; Joy 2019; Mattsson 2006; Mehrotra 2010; Murphy et al. 2009; Nayak and Robbins 2018). As one of the core tenets of intersectionality is to capture the complex ways that multiple disadvantages come together, the intersectionality wheel has the potential to stimulate interest and actively engage students to develop their understandings of how systemic inequalities and relations of power manifest for diverse individuals and groups. In this sense, the intersectionality wheel will challenge students to move away from the individualisation of social problems, while simultaneously bringing into view the structural intersections of various social categories such as race, class, gender, sexual orientation, age, disability, or religious beliefs that come together to frame experiences (Krumer-Nevo and Komem 2015). In short, the intersectionality wheel can be an effective tool to enrich students' understanding of how multiple systems of oppression are enmeshed and mutually reinforcing (May 2015), to consider the implications of what this means for the lived experiences of service users they will encounter in practice.

Discussion point

• How can the intersectionality wheel help you to understand your own positionality and social location?

Intersectional pedagogy for anti-oppressive practice

So far, this chapter has focused on the intersectionality wheel, which shows the overlapping forms of oppressions. In the next section, I will focus on another pedagogical tool that can be used with social work students, notably, Case's (2017) intersectional pedagogy model, to suggest strategies that can be used for anti-oppressive pedagogy and practice. The intersectional pedagogy model was created by Case for developing best practices for effective teaching and learning about intersections of identity. Case's conceptual framework offers some tools which can be used to build on the work started with the intersectionality wheel to push the boundaries of teaching about oppression and the intersection of various identities. The following is an elaboration of Case's ten elements that are essential for operationalising intersectionality in the classroom.

1. *Conceptualises intersectionality as a complex analysis of both privileged and oppressed social identities.*

As anti-oppressive scholarship has consistently shown, critically engaging with debates about privileged and oppressed social identities in social work necessitates foregrounding issues of power, oppression, and structural inequalities (Abrams and Molo 2009; Dominelli 1988; Krumer-Nevo and Komem 2015; Singh and Masocha 2020). It can therefore be argued that an intersectional lens helps us to understand that identity has to be conceptualised in ways that take account of multiple and intersecting forms of oppressions (e.g., racism, sexism, classism, heterosexism, disabilism, ageism). The important point here is that incorporating intersectional approaches can engender a transformative learning environment that will cultivate and enrich a complex understanding of different forms of oppression. This is crucial, as intersectional frames of analyses can serve as a springboard to bring to the surface the implicit values and expectations that arise when we consider multiple identities and oppressions. Perhaps most obviously, an intersectional lens offers the possibilities to stimulate curiosity in learners to unpack ideas and debates about individual and group identities and their relevance for social work. Most notably, intersectionality provides the necessary analytical tools to capture the complexities of how multiple axes of identities combine to frame experiences of oppression. Indeed, an intersectional approach is a useful way of having a critical exploration of how different forms of inequity combine with and intensify oppression for individuals and communities with whom social workers practice.

2. Teaches intersectionality across a wide variety of oppressions.

Using intersectionality as a pedagogical approach can provide an entry point for students to begin to explore multiple forms of oppression. This is particularly important for facilitating discussions about oppression without privileging one form of oppression over another. Ultimately, the goal is to avoid debates about which group is more oppressed, to essentially resist the equality of oppressions perspective (Schiele 2007). Eschewing what Audre Lorde (1983, 9) refers to as the hierarchy of oppressions trope is essential. With an intersectional lens we are able to have more nuanced discussion about the compounding effects of many sites of oppression such as racism, classism, sexism, homophobia, ageism, and disablism, that combine to frame the material and relational experiences of minority groups (Krumer-Nevo and Komem 2015; Mattsson 2014; Smith and Shin 2015). Crucially, teaching intersectionality across a wide range of oppressions offers a way of thinking about core concepts concerning inclusion and exclusion, deserving and undeserving, and the power relationships that service users with multiple stigmatised identities have to navigate in the welfare system. As Macey and Moxon (1996) assert, there is a crucial need to have alternative frameworks that can adequately navigate the complexity of the issues concerning different forms of oppression. Put simply, intersectionality as a pedagogical method can allow us to look at different forms of oppressions by offering a way to identify a number of discriminations and disadvantages to foster social justice-oriented classrooms (Smele et al. 2017).

3. Aims to uncover invisible intersections.

As an organising framework, intersectionality helps to remind us at all times of the need to be sensitive to the less visible aspects of identities that people bring, but also to recognise that there are hidden intersections that need to be made visible. For example, people with multiple stigmatised identities such as being transgender, HIV positive, or having mental health problems, uncertain immigration status, or indeed hidden intellectual disabilities, will most definitely intersect in complex ways with their racialised, gendered, or classed identities. As the society becomes more diverse, so the issues that emerge become more complex. Arguably, engaging questions of difference can result in a better understanding of hidden aspects of identities and the unique forms of discrimination that are created as a result. An important teaching and learning technique is to create inclusivity in the classroom as this will provide a space for participatory learning to amplify the voices of those with more marginalised social identities (Taylor Yates and Rai 2019). Given the importance of reflection in social work, providing spaces for students and practitioners to explore discomforting issues will also create possibilities to interrogate marginalising perspectives and experiences that may result in some intersections being more visible than others.

4. *Includes privilege as an essential aspect of learning about intersectionality.*

It is important that students recognise different forms of privilege (e.g., race, class, gender, and economic privilege), to acknowledge and reflect on their own privilege. McIntosh (1989) utilised the metaphor the invisible knapsack to elaborate the ways that psychological and material benefits of 'white privilege' manifest. Whiteness is defined by McIntosh as a set of assumptions and beliefs that reify the interests and outlooks of white people as the norm (McIntosh 1989). Certainly, social work education does not have a strong track record of engaging with whiteness (Davis and Gentlewarrior 2015; Jeyasingham 2012). Indeed, Tascón and Ife (2020) argue that white social workers must be able to unpack the whiteness of the knowledge they bring to their practice. Moreover, white students and indeed educators may not recognise white privilege and the advantages that flow from it. Hence, there is growing awareness that helping students address unacknowledged white privilege should be a key component of teaching about racism (Heller 2010). It is also crucial to consider that learning about privilege and oppression may engender defensive and resistant behaviours. While these challenges are inevitable, an intersectional approach is well versed to engage with the complexities of systems of oppression, to understand how privilege is experienced in a context of racism, sexism, classism, and heterosexism. In this sense, intersectionality enables students from minority backgrounds to construct counternarratives to challenge the existing assumptions rooted in whiteness that Western and Eurocentric forms of knowledge are the only valid ways of knowing (Bernard 2017). Thus, an intersectional lens is crucial for the unpacking of privileged identities and, in particular, it offers a way to understand how different kinds of privilege such as racial and class privilege operate to shore up power and oppression.

5. *Analyses power in teaching about intersectional theory.*

An intersectional pedagogical approach provides an important jumping off point for understanding power relations in social work practice. How power is exercised in social work practice is something that needs greater attention for effective anti-oppressive practice. Intersectionality as an analytical tool offers the means to unpack structures of power and unfair power relationships for advancing human rights and social justice (Robinson et al. 2016). Intersectionality's primary concern with oppressions thus provides an ideal framework for critiquing the inherent power relationships in social work. As Bundy-Fazioli et al. (2013) argue, it is vital that educators facilitate the development of students' critical skills for engaging more fully with the workings of power imbalances in social work practice, including their own situated power. It is important for social workers to recognise the power that they represent and creating learning opportunities to engage with these issues will enhance students' understanding of different forms of power and the complexities of relations of power and powerlessness (Tew 2006). Undoubtedly, power is complex and contradictory for social workers. As Smith (2008) points out, power is an issue that is central to every aspect of social workers' practice, which causes some discomfort to practitioners, who are acutely aware of their own relative powerlessness in an organisational and structural sense, even as they have to manage their own authority over service users. But perhaps more importantly, an intersectionality-informed approach to power better captures the complexities of power relations that pervade much social work practice.

6. *Involves educator personal reflection on intersecting identities, biases, and assumptions.*

Educators must not underestimate the importance of being able to understand how their own positionality impacts their teaching and the classroom environment. If educators are to stimulate students' reflections of multiple oppressions such as racism, homophobia, and gendered power relationships, as well as their own lived experiences of oppression, they must be able to reflect on their own identities, privilege, and imbalances of power (Fook and Gardner 2007). In particular, educators need to be able to interrogate how they acknowledge and understand their own biases in relation to race, gender, age, sexual orientation, disability, class, or religious beliefs to consider how such elements influence their pedagogical practices. Most crucially, educators must be explicitly aware of their positionality in order to acknowledge their personal biases and understand how they bring these biases to their teaching. For example, drawing on insights from Palmer's (2007) *The Courage to Teach*, Gates (2011, 72) argues that effective educators must be able to 'build relationships with students and present themselves as authentic human beings'. According to Gates, authenticity and wholeness are central to effective teaching and learning. In short, employing intersectionality as a teaching methodology (Smele et al. 2017) is ideal for educators to reflect on their own identities in order to create classroom environments where students feel safe enough to engage in difficult conversations about inequalities and oppression.

7. *Encourages student reflection and writing about their own intersecting identities.*

The significance of a safe environment to explore which categories of identities students ascribe to themselves is critically important for students positioned within marginalised and devalued social identities. Thus, intersectional teaching can provide a lens for students to interrogate their own intersecting identities and, in particular, the myriad ways their identities may be constructed. For instance, some students may find it challenging to be asked to identify what is the most important facet of their identity. Smele et al. (2017) emphasise that to really interrogate multiple layers of identities when teaching about intersectionality, it is critical to embrace vulnerability, discomfort, and the possibility of conflict in classrooms. Therefore, pedagogical approaches that are intersectional can enrich the learning opportunities for students to reflect on their subjectivities and positionalities. Employing an intersectional lens offers opportunities to probe the manifestations of oppressions and the impact of different components on identity. A particularly striking element of intersectionality is that it offers the conceptual resources to penetrate power relations to capture the nuances surrounding multiple and shifting identities and critical self-awareness.

8. *Promotes social action to dismantle oppression.*

An intersectional perspective chimes with one of the core values of social work that emphasises promoting empowerment and social justice. The significance of having tools to dismantle oppression and advance a social justice-oriented practice is something that is advocated by a number of social work scholars (Brown 2012; Gatenio Gabel and Mapp 2019; Havig 2013; Ferguson and Smith 2012; Nicotera 2019). In the current climate, where a neoliberalist agenda and managerialism models of service delivery predominate (Ferguson and Smith 2012), there are significant challenges for advancing social justice-oriented practice (Fenton 2016; Fenton 2018). But what matters here is that social workers are uniquely situated to bear witness to the devastating impact of neoliberal environments on welfare services (Bernard 2017). Case's (2017) notion of promoting social action to dismantle oppression through student learning that extends beyond the classroom is an excellent way to deploy intersectionality as theory and praxis.

Prior to starting their social work studies, some students would have been politically active and involved in social movements and other forms of activism. For example, student activism in social movements and campaigning organisations such as Social Work Action Network (SWAN), a radical and campaigning organisation, and Social Work Without Borders, who promote activism with asylum seekers and refugees, are good examples of how student activists can find platforms to utilise intersectionality principles. For instance, an intersectional framework can enable engagement with the contextual and structural factors that contribute to service users' lived experiences which are rooted in social inequalities and oppression. Specifically, intersectionality's commitment to social justice and social change provides social workers with the necessary tools for challenging oppression and developing emancipatory approaches, such as feminist, critical race theory, rights-based, and anti-oppressive approaches to social work. Anti-oppressive practice can help reduce some of the barriers that service users experience, and the teaching of anti-oppressive principles has a vital role to play because it offers progressive possibilities and will encourage students to engage with the difficult questions of oppression and privilege.

9.   *Values the voices of the marginalised and oppressed.*

Centring the voices of multiple oppressed individuals and groups is important but brings its own set of challenges. As previously mentioned, it will be important not to fall into the trap of the hierarchy of oppressions trope, and by implication, the hierarchy of voice. As the classroom becomes more diverse, comprised of students with multiple identities, there are barriers to the inclusion of marginalised and devalued voices (Chi-Pun Liu 2017). As argued by Bailey and Mobley (2019), we need to be attentive to the ways that ableism impacts experiences and can result in the exclusion and marginalisation of disabled people's voices. With regards to racialised identities and experiences, some white educators and students may be uncomfortable with discussing race, while some may struggle to acknowledge white privilege, and generally avoid conversations about race and racism. Moreover, debates about non-binary gender identity, gender fluidity, and gender variance illuminate other aspects of the diversity and complexities of identities (Smith and Shin 2015).

Certainly, it is important and necessary to consider the ways that students who are themselves from oppressed groups can be oppressive to other minority groups in the context of religion and faith. For example, the *Diversity and Progression* research identified that some black students with strong religious beliefs resisted teachings about same-sex relationships and used their religion as a justification for extolling homophobic views (Bernard et al. 2014). In this case we can see the privileging of race over sexual orientation, taking place within different marginalised groups.

Therefore, in crucial ways, there are some challenges to navigate to create inclusive spaces where all voices are valued, when there are competing inequalities. As Case (2017) makes clear, as course content begins to challenge long-held values, tradition, and beliefs, students may experience hopelessness, guilt, anger, frustration, defensiveness, and cognitive dissonance. What is important to emphasise here is that the classroom is a space of struggle that can be used to engage in debates about different ways of knowing and confronting uncomfortable truths (Smele et al. 2017).

Intersectionality as an analytical tool enables us to ask difficult questions, such as: whose voices are given centre stage? Whose voices are absent? Whose voices are marginalised and devalued? And what are the barriers to finding your own voice? As bell hooks (1988) asserts, moving from silence into speech is a gesture of resistance, an affirmation of struggle. Intersectionality thus offers a way for marginalised learners to find a voice.

10. Infuses intersectional studies across the curriculum.

As previously mentioned, intersectionality has relevance and applicability to a wide range of subjects, topics, and fields of practice. Intersectionality also reminds us that a culturally inclusive curriculum should reflect the history and culture of students of all backgrounds. Because intersectional approaches are concerned with the breath of human experiences (Murphy et al. 2009), intersectionality opens up possibilities for unpacking the dominant ideas, assumptions and theoretical groundings that underpin the knowledge-bases of much social work practice (Bubar et al. 2016; Busche et al. 2012).

A core part of social work education and training is concerned with asking critical questions about social inequalities, oppression, discrimination, and diversity. Indeed, a key goal is for social workers to be able to incorporate an integrated understanding of oppression into their practice (Keating 2000). In one sense, the movement of decolonising social work forces us to look more critically at the Eurocentric values, traditions, and paradigms that permeate much social work practice and education and to deploy alternative ways of knowing (Choate 2019; Grey et al. 2016; Rowe et al. 2015; Singh and Masocha 2020; Schmid and Morgenshtern 2019). In short, infusing intersectional approaches throughout the curriculum will help create an important organising principle for assisting students in their knowledge development for anti-oppressive practice.

Reflective questions

- What are your reflections on Case's ten-point model of intersectional pedagogy?
- How do you think your experience of education has been influenced by your identity?
- How has your identity as a woman/man/non-binary/LGBTQI affected your life experiences to date?
- What are some of the enablers and barriers for addressing privilege and oppression in the classroom?
- What are some of the enablers and barriers for addressing and challenging deep-rooted beliefs about privilege and oppression in the classroom?

Conclusion

This chapter has set out some of the ways that intersectionality can be employed to develop critical pedagogy for learning about power, oppression, and privilege. As such, it has served to highlight how the intersectionality wheel can help lay the foundation to facilitate a contextualisation of systems of oppressions, whilst the intersectional pedagogy model offers a practical tool for putting the analytical framework offered by intersectionality into practice in the social work classroom.

Importantly, an intersectional perspective offers some powerful conceptual and analytical tools for enabling difficult conversations to take place about oppressions in its micro and macro contexts. To that end, intersectionality provides us with some strategies necessary for fostering participatory learning classrooms to enable students to connect theory to their lived experiences, as well as to understand the experiences of people with marginalised social identities. Taken together, the intersectionality wheel and the intersectional pedagogy model provide tools to help us interrogate the sites of oppression for effective teaching and learning to tackle social inequalities.

References

Abrams, Laura S., and Molo, Jene A. 2009. Critical race theory and the cultural competence dilemma in social work education. *Journal of Social Work Education* 45 (2): 245–261.

Ahmad Bandana. 1990. *Black Perspectives in Social Work*. Birmingham: Venture Press.

Aymer, Cathy. 2002. The dilemmas for black social work professionals: Therapeutic implications. *Journal of Social Work Practice* 16 (1): 15–21.

Bailey, Moya, and Izetta A. Mobley. 2019. Work in the intersections: A black feminist disability framework. *Gender and Society* 33 (1): 19–40.

Beltran, Ramona, and Gita Mehrotra. 2015. Honoring our intellectual ancestors: A feminist of color treaty for creating allied collaboration. *Affilia* 30 (1): 106–116.

Bernard, Claudia. Anna Fairtlough, Joan Fletcher and Akile Ahmet. 2014. A qualitative study of marginalised social work students' views of social work education and learning. *British Journal of Social Work* 44 (7): 1934–1949.

Bernard, Claudia. 2017. Reflecting on a journey: Positionality, marginality and the outsider-within. In *Inside the Ivory Tower: Narratives of Women of Colour Surviving and Thriving in British Academia*, eds. Deborah Gabriel and Shirley Ann Tate, 88–90. London: Trentham Books.

Bernard, Claudia. 2019. Using an intersectional lens to examine the child sexual exploitation of black adolescents. In *Child Sexual Exploitation: Why Theory Matters*, ed. Jenny Pearce, 193–208, Bristol: Policy Press.

Bhatti-Sinclair, Kish. 2011. *Anti-racist Practice in Social Work*. Basingstoke: Palgrave Macmillan.

Brown, Catrina G. 2012. Anti-oppression through a postmodern lens: Dismantling the master's conceptual tools in discursive social work practice. *Critical Social Work* 13 (1): 34–65.

Bubar, Roe, Karina Cespedes, and Kimberly Bundy-Fazioli. 2016. Intersectionality and social work: Omissions of race, class, and sexuality in graduate school education. *Journal of Social Work Education* 52 (3): 283–296.

Bundy-Fazioli, Kimberly, Louise M. Quijano, and Roe Bubar. 2013. Graduate students' perceptions of professional power in social work practice. *Journal of Social Work Education* 49 (1): 108–121.

Busche, Mart, Elli Scambor, and Olaf Stuve. 2012. An intersectional perspective in social work and education. *ERIS Web Journal* 1: 2–14.

Case, K. A. 2017. *Intersectional Pedagogy: Complicating Identity and Social Justice.* London: Routledge.

Chi-Pun Liu, Ben. 2017. Intersectional impact of multiple identities of social work education in the UK. *Journal of Social Work* 17 (2): 226–242.

Choate, Peter W. 2019. The call to decolonise: Social work's challenge for working with indigenous peoples. *British Journal of Social Work* 49 (4): 1081–1099.

Davis, Ashley, and Sabrina Gentlewarrior. 2015. White privilege and clinical social work practice: Reflections and recommendations. *Journal of Progressive Human Services* 26 (3): 191–208.

DiAngelo, Robin J., and Özlem Sensoy. 2014. Leaning in: A student's guide to engaging constructively with social justice content. *Radical Pedagogy* 11 (1): 1–15.

Dominelli, Lena. 1988. *Anti-racist Social Work*. London: Macmillan.

Dunk-West, Priscilla and Trish Hafford-Lethfield. 2011. *Sexual Identities and Sexuality in Social Work*. Farnham: Ashgate.

Fenton, Jane. 2016. *Values in Social Work: Reconnecting with Social Justice.* Basingstoke: Palgrave MacMillan.

Fenton, Jane. 2018. Putting old heads on young shoulders: Helping social work students uncover the neoliberal hegemony. *Social Work Education* 37 (8): 941–954.

Ferguson, Iain, and Linda Smith. 2012. Education for change: Student placements in campaigning organisations and social movements in South Africa. *British Journal of Social Work* 42 (5): 974–994.

Fook, Jan and Fiona Gardner. 2007. *Practicing Critical Reflection.* Maidenhead: Open University Press.

Gatenio Gabel, Shirley, and Susan Mapp. 2019. Teaching human rights and social justice in social work education. *Journal of Social Work Education*, 56 (3): 428–441.

Gates, Trevor G. 2011. Coming out in the social work classroom: Reclaiming wholeness and finding the teacher within. *Social Work Education* 30 (1): 70–82.

Graham, Mekada and Jerome H. Schiele. 2010. Equality-of-oppressions and anti-discriminatory models in social work: Reflections from the USA and UK. *European Journal of Social Work* 13 (2): 231–244.

Gray, Mel, John Coates, Michael Yellow Bird, and Tiani Hetherington. 2016. *Decolonizing Social Work.* London: Routledge.

Griffin, Cindy L., and Karma R. Chávez. 2012. Standing in the intersections of feminism, intersectionality, and communication studies. In *Standing in the Intersection: Feminist Voices, Feminist Practices in Communication Studies*, eds. Cindy L. Griffin and Karma R. Chávez, 1–31. Albany, NY: State University of New York Press.

Havig, Kirsten. 2013. Empowering students to promote social justice: A qualitative study of field instructor' perceptions and strategies. *Field Educator* 3 (2): 1–24.

Heller, Jennifer. 2010. Emerging themes on aspects of social class and the discourse of white privilege. *Journal of Intercultural Studies* 31 (1): 111–120.

Hicks, Stephen. 2008. Thinking through sexuality. *Journal of Social Work* 8 (1): 65–82.

hooks, bell. 1988. *Talking Back: Thinking Feminist, Thinking Black.* Boston, MA: South End Press.

hooks, bell. 1994. *Teaching to Transgress: Education as the Practice of Freedom*. New York: Routledge.

Hudson, Kimberly D., and Evette J. Richardson. 2016. Centering power, positionality, and emotional labor in a Master of Social Work research course: Perspectives from a student and instructor. *Qualitative Social Work* 15 (3): 414–427.

Jeyasingham, Dharman. 2012. White noise: A critical evaluation of social work education's engagement with whiteness studies. *British Journal of Social Work* 42 (4): 669–686.

Joy, Eileen. 2019. 'You cannot take it with you': Reflections on intersectionality and social work. *Aotearoa New Zealand Social Work* 37 (1): 42–48.

Keating, Frank. 2000. Anti-racist perspectives: What are the gains for social work? *Social Work Education* 19 (1): 77–87.

Krumer-Nevo, Michal, and Michal Komem. 2015. Intersectionality and critical social work with girls: Theory and practice. *British Journal of Social Work* 45 (4): 1190–1206.

Kosteciki, Tina. 2016. Developing anti-ageist practice in social work. In *Doing Critical Social Work: Transformative Practices for Social Justice*, eds. Bob Pease, Sophie Goldingay, Norah Hosken, and Sharlene Nipperess, 241–253. Crows Nest, NSW: Allen & Unwin.

Lorde, Audre. 1983. There is no hierarchy of oppressions. *Interracial Books for Children Bulletin* 14 (3–4): 9.

Macey, Marie, and Eileen Moxon. 1996. An examination of anti-racist and anti-oppressive theory and practice in social work education. *British Journal of Social Work* 26 (3): 297–314.

Mattsson, Tina. 2014. Intersectionality as a useful tool: Anti-oppressive social work and critical reflection. *Affilia* 29 (1): 8–17.

May, Vivian M. 2015. *Pursing Intersectionality, Unsettling Dominant Imaginaries*. New York: Routledge.

McIntosh, Peggy. 1989. White privilege: Unpacking the invisible knapsack. *Peace and Freedom*. July/August 1989.

Mehrotra, Gita. 2010. Toward a continuum of intersectionality theorizing for feminist social work scholarship. *Affilia* 25 (4): 417–430.

Murphy, Yvette, Valerie Hunt, Anna M. Zajicek, Adele N. Norris, and Leah Hamilton. 2009. *Incorporating Intersectionality in Social*

Work Practice, Research, Policy and Education. Washington DC: NASW.

Nicotera, Anthony. 2019. Social justice and social work, a fierce urgency: Recommendations for social work social justice pedagogy. *Journal of Social Work Education* 55 (3): 460–475.

Palmer, Parker J. 2007. *The Courage to Teach: Exploring the Inner Landscape of a Teacher's Life*, 10th anniversary edn. San Francisco: Jossey-Bass.

Phillips, Ruth and Viviene E. Cree. 2014. What does the 'fourth wave' mean for teaching feminism in twenty-first century social work? *Social Work Education* 33 (7): 930–943.

Robinson, Michael A., Bronwyn Cross-Denny, Karen Kyeunghae Lee, Lisa Marie Werkmeister Rozas, and Ann-Marie Yamada. 2016. Teaching note: Teaching intersectionality: Transforming cultural competence content in social work education. *Journal of Social Work Education* 52 (4): 509–517.

Rowe, Simone, Eileen Baldry, and Wendy Earles. 2015. Decolonising social work research: Learning from critical indigenous approaches. *Australian Social Work* 68 (3): 296–308.

Schiele, Jerome H. 2007. Implications of the equality-of-oppressions paradigm for curriculum content on people of color. *Journal of Social Work Education* 43 (1): 83–100.

Schmid, Jeanette, and Marina Morgenshtern. 2019. Pulling together the threads: Current understandings of contextualized social work education. *Critical Social Work* 20 (1): 67–86.

Shuttleworth, Russell. 2016. Social work, disability and social change: a critical participatory approach. In *Doing Critical Social Work: Transformative Practices for Social Justice*, eds. Bob Pease, Sophie Goldingay, Norah Hosken, and Sharlene Nipperess, 298–309. Crows Nest, NSW: Allen & Unwin.

Simpson, Joanna. 2009. *Everyone Belongs: A Toolkit for Applying Intersectionality.* Ottawa: CRIAW/ICREF.

Singh, Gurnam, and Shepard and Masocha. 2020. *Anti-racist Social Work: International Perspectives.* London: London: Red Globe Press.

Smele, Sandra, Rehanna Siew-Sarju, Elena Chou, Pat Breton, and Nicole S. Bernhardt. 2017. Intersectional pedagogical practices in the context of the neoliberal diversity regime. *Teaching in Higher Education* 22 (6): 690–704.

Smethurst, Christopher and Kish Bhatti-Sinclair. 2017. Diversity and difference in challenging times: The social and political context, in *Diversity, Difference and Dilemmas: Analysing Concepts and Developing Skills*, eds. Kish Bhatti-Sinclair and Christopher Smethurst, 3–12. London: Open University Press.

Smith, Lance C., and Richard Q. Shin. 2015. Negotiating the intersection of racial oppression and heteronormativity. *Journal of Homosexuality* 62 (11): 1459–1484.

Smith, Roger. 2008. *Social Work and Power*. Basingstoke: Palgrave Macmillan.

Tascón, Sonia M., and Jim Ife. 2020. *Disrupting Whiteness in Social Work*. New York: Routledge.

Taylor Yates, Helen, and Abha Rai. 2019. A scoping review of feminism in U.S. social work education: Strategies and implications for the contemporary classroom. *Journal of Evidence-Informed Social Work* 16 (2): 117–129.

Tew, Jerry. 2006. Understanding power and powerlessness: Towards a framework for emancipatory practice in social work. *Journal of Social Work* 6 (1): 33–51.

Williams, Charlotte. 1999. Connecting anti-racist and anti-oppressive theory and practice: Retrenchment or reappraisal? *British Journal of Social Work* 29 (2): 211–230.

Williams, Charlotte. 2016. Social work and the challenge of race equality. In *Routledge International Handbook of Social Work Education*, eds. Imogen Taylor, Marion Bogo, Michelle Lefevre, and Barbra Teater, 14–26. Abingdon: Routledge.

7 Intersectional approaches and social work research

This chapter examines intersectional approaches to social work research. It is broadly acknowledged that social workers need to have a critical understanding of research, to know how to evaluate research findings to integrate research knowledge and skills into their practice; I suggest that it is also crucial for social workers to be able to evaluate research drawing on critical perspectives. Therefore, in this chapter, my aim is to describe some key principles of intersectionality to help students better understand the practical applications of research. In the first section, I will outline how an intersectional approach can be used to interpret and understand research, as well as to undertake original research. In the second, I will draw on some examples from research projects I have undertaken to show the practical applications of conducting intersectional research.

Research teaching and learning in social work education

The teaching of research skills on social work programmes has been well covered in social work education literature (see Blakemore and Howard 2015; Cameron and Este 2008; Einbinder 2014; Fish 2015; Lyons 2000; Sharland and Teater 2016; Shaw 2007; Teater et al. 2017; Whittaker 2012). Indeed, the Knowledge and Skills Statement (KSS) for child and family work and adult services stipulates that social workers should be able to use evidence from research to inform their practice (Department for Education 2018). Thus, the need for social work practitioners to be able to acquire a basic introduction to methodological concepts and procedures, and to be able to engage with research as well as produce research is widely acknowledged, and the importance of cultivating research-mindedness for enabling

DOI: 10.4324/9780429467288-7

students to have a critical appreciation of research and build capacity has been strongly emphasised (Einbinder 2014; Humphries 2008). Various authors advocate the teaching of quantitative and qualitative methodologies so that practitioners can engage with the practical application of research (Cameron and Este 2008; Hardwick and Worsley 2011; Smith 2009). As Teater et al. (2017) put it, research has an important role to play in helping to improve social workers' understandings of the behaviours, experiences, and contextual nature of services users' day-to-day lives. Yet, it should be noted that there are key challenges to teaching research skills to social work students (Teater et al. 2017). It has also been noted that social work students often find learning about research methods intimidating and many struggle to understand key research concepts and their application to practice (Einbinder 2014; Kiik 2005; Whittaker 2012). However, as Hardwick and Worsley (2011) highlight, the teaching of research-mindedness develops a practitioner's ability to use research to inform their practice, and to identify critical issues for further enquiry.

Approaches to intersectionality and social work research

In Chapter 2, I outlined some of the ways that intersectionality is increasingly being used in social work education and training for learning about structural disadvantages and empowerment. Nevertheless, in the UK, the relevance of intersectionality to social work research has been much less considered in the literature. Yet, there is a growing body of social work research where intersectionality forms a key component of the methodological approach (Murphy et al. 2009), such as Krumer-Nevo and Komem's (2013) research using intersectionality as a guiding framework for examining social work practice with multiply marginalised girls in Israel, and Hulko's (2004) systematic investigation into the subjective experiences of dementia in later life, which utilised an intersectional methodology. Additionally, Hulko and Hovanes (2018) drew on intersectionality as a methodological framing to explore the experiences and perspectives of diverse women who identify as sexual and/or gender minorities. Furthermore, the work of Drummond and Brotman (2014) and Brotman et al. (2020) are examples of an intersectional life-course approach to narrative inquiry. For example, Brotman et al. (2020, 467) used an intersectional life-course approach to explore the lives of racialised young women from immigrant families to understand the role of gender, racialisation, and migration in shaping their lived experiences of care. These pieces of research offer insights into how intersectional approaches can be incorporated into social work research for conceptualising experiences of marginality that arise in social work practice (Hulko and Hovanes 2018). As Atewologun and Ramaswami (2018) remind us, intersectionality is a critical tool for capturing socially constituted everyday experiences at the nexus of structures of power. Crucially, the important point here is that a key goal of social work research should be to develop critical research that aims to improve the lives of service users. As Hill Collins and Bilge (2016) point out, in a discipline like social work that has a strong applied focus, theory and practice are very interconnected, and an intersectional lens can influence the themes, questions, and concerns that social work researchers address.

As I indicated in Chapter 2, intersectionality resonates with social work's core principles of social justice, human rights, collective responsibility and respect for diversities (IFSW 2014). As an applied justice-oriented discipline, social work is attentive to the contextual nature of service users' lives and strives for an empowerment-based and emancipatory practice (Lavalette et al. 2020). Indeed, intersectionality is a central tool for understanding the experiences of multiply marginalised and oppressed groups, principles that are integral to social work practice (Murphy et al. 2009).

Precisely because the lives of the individuals, groups, and communities that social workers typically work with are often embedded in multiple layers of disadvantage, intersectionality offers us new ways to interrogate these factors. It follows, then, that intersectionality as an organising framework is valuable for social work researchers because it provides a means for understanding everyday experiences that are significantly impacted by systemic inequalities. Additionally, and more importantly, intersectionality not only provides a theoretical lens for capturing and recognising multiple categories of inequalities used in research, it also enables more nuanced interpretations of the interconnectedness of various forms of oppressions that work in tandem (Bowleg 2008).

Though intersectionality is much more present in the work of practitioners utilising qualitative research methods (Abrams et al. 2020; Atewologun and Mahalingam 2018; Brotman et al. 2020; Windsong 2018), it is becoming increasingly popular in quantitative and mixed-methods research (Bailey et al. 2019; Bauer and Schiem 2019; Codiroli Mcmaster and Cook 2019; Else-Quest and Hyde 2016; Fehrenbacher and Patel 2020; Grace 2014; Syed 2010). As mentioned earlier, a major attraction is that intersectionality is well-suited to different forms of enquiry that need to take account of multifaceted lived experiences that are deeply embedded in interlocking systems of oppression (Bailey et al. 2019; Bowleg and Bauer 2016; Choo and Ferree 2010; Cole 2009; Else-Quest and Hyde 2016; Windsong 2018). As has been described by a number of scholars, intersectional approaches can be useful because as well as providing researchers with an explanatory framework for forms of analysis and interpretation of data, it provides possibilities to probe much more deeply into the complex manifestations of intersectional dynamics because it offers multiple sites of entry (Bernard 2019; Clarke and McCall 2013; Cole 2009; Hillsburg 2013; Rice et al. 2019; Warner 2008).

To be clear, though there are many scholars who extol the benefits and opportunities of an intersectional approach to research, one of the ongoing debates concerns the methodological challenges of conducting empirical research in the absence of a methodology of intersectionality (see for example, Bailey et al. 2019; Bowleg and Bauer 2016: Choo and Ferree 2010; Cho et al. 2013; Grace 2014; Hillsburg 2013; McCall 2005; Naples 2009; Rice et al. 2019; Windsong 2018). In particular, how to analyse intersections, and which intersections to include in analyses, are questions that arise in debates (Hillsburg 2013; McCall 2005). We are reminded by Rice et al. (2019)

that intersectionality is applied in varying ways; some scholars see it as a theoretical or methodological approach, whilst others use it as an interpretive tool and framing strategy for social analysis. The point has been made elsewhere that intersectionality lacks a clearly defined methodology (Davis, 2008). As stated by Murphy et al. (2009), the lack of a clear set of methodological procedures and techniques for doing intersectional research means there are some challenges when utilising it for social work, though within the field, some scholars argue that intersectionality's analytical strategies can provide a set of tools to identify the concepts that are germane for understanding the confluence of experiences rooted in discrimination and disadvantages (Krumer-Nevo and Komem 2013; Murphy et al. 2009).

Essentially, applying intersectionality to social work research provides the means to expose the complex manifestations of the diverse array of issues such as poverty, socio-economic inequalities, homelessness, gender-based violence, mental ill-health, and health disparities, among others, that give rise to the personal troubles that bring individuals and families to the attention of social workers. In this regard, Cole (2009, 171) usefully provides a helpful set of questions that researchers must answer in order to facilitate an application of intersectional research: (1) Who is included within this category? (2) What role does inequality play? (3) Where are there similarities? (4) Whose experiences are at the centre of the analysis? We can see here that Cole recognises that an intersectional framework in research offers important insights into the processes of research and the significance of social categories as signifying hierarchies of power and privilege that shape social and material circumstances. Or, simply put, the analytical framework provided by intersectionality for critical research in social work allows for an interrogation of the dynamic and complex processes of social experiences for those with multiply marginalised identities (Bowleg 2008).

I will now explore the application of intersectionality to research, sharing some examples of how intersectionality can be utilised to shape research questions and develop analyses by drawing on two research projects.

Case study 1

The research that formed the basis of the book *Constructing Lived Experiences: Representations of Black Mothers in Child Sexual Abuse Discourses* (Bernard 2001) is a qualitative study that investigated black mothers' responses to the sexual abuse of their children. A central aim of this research was to critically examine the issues framing black mothers' emotional and behavioural responses in the aftermath of the sexual abuse of their children to understand their help-seeking behaviours. The rationale for this research was that in child protection social work at that time, dominant heteronormative assumptions about ideal mothers often resulted in attributing blame to mothers for failing to protect their children. Therefore, centring the lived experiences of black mothers in this research was, in some ways, important as in previous research scant attention had been paid to the ways that deficit discourses about black families intersect with mother-blaming narratives to shape black mothers' responses. Because of these concerns, the purpose of this study was to shed light on black mothers' experiences of parenting in the aftermath of abuse, to generate new knowledge of the racialised gendered experiences of non-abusing black mothers to expand the thinking more deeply to improve social work interventions with black families.

The study adopted a qualitative methodology and, through a series of semi-structured, in-depth individual interviews with 30 black mothers of Caribbean and African backgrounds whose children had experienced intrafamilial and extrafamilial sexual abuse, I collected rich data. The interviews explored how the mothers articulated the processes of disclosure and coping behaviours. The analysis of the data utilised techniques and procedures from grounded theory methodology. As a methodological tool for data analysis, grounded theory is useful for constructing theory from data that is embedded in lived experiences that are interpretive (Charmaz 1995; Strauss and Corbin 1998). Taken together as theoretical guides, grounded theory and intersectionality helped me in conceptualising the complex interplay of cultural, emotional, and psychological processes underpinning black mothers' experiences, to illuminate the meanings and coping behaviours they adopted.

Because I wanted to capture how multiple identity markers (e.g., race, gender, and class) overlap and interact to shape the mothers' responses, intersectionality served as a useful conceptual tool to untangle the critical factors shaping and impacting their responses to the abuse of their children. More specifically, intersectionality served as a framing by providing an important lens through which to interpret the relational and contextual nature of the mothers' particular experiences to understand how they navigated the complex terrain of multiple forms of oppression that shaped their responses to their children's victimisation. From this vantage point, the mothers' emotional and behavioural responses cannot be decontextualised from the sociocultural context within which their lived experiences are situated.

At the core of the concern was to unpack what was going on emotionally, psychologically, and practically for the mothers. Significant here is that an intersectional approach guided the analytical process to enable me to build the line of arguments I advanced about the complicated choices the mothers faced. It is important to stress that the theme of conflict of loyalties arose in five interconnected strands: (1) Conflict in the mother-child relationship; (2) Familial conflict; (3) Conflictual feelings towards their husband/partner; (4) Conflict with self; and (5) Conflict about using child protection services (Bernard 2013). Crucially, within an intersectional frame of reference, I was able to analyse these broad categories to develop the overarching theme of divided loyalties. Essentially, by placing the basic tenet of intersectionality at the heart of the research (namely, the simultaneity of oppression concept), enabled me to uncover some of the essential elements of the complex networks of relationships within which the mothers' kinship ties are embedded, to foreground how conflictual loyalties are generated for black mothers. What is perhaps most important to stress is that I developed the concept of divided loyalty to unravel the emotional and behavioural responses of the mothers. This is perhaps because the effects of the abuse on the mothers' parenting needed to be made visible for a more nuanced understanding of the particular ways their mothering roles are impacted in the aftermath of the sexual abuse of their children. Engaging with intersectionality therefore offered a useful way of conceptualising the multifaceted nature of the mothers' emotional and behavioural responses to delve into the layers of complexities and inherent contradictions arising as a result of competing loyalties and conflictual relationships because their experiences were situated within mutually reinforcing oppressions. Thus, from the perspective of intersectionality, it was crucial to analyse the convergence of race and gender to elucidate the meanings associated with the emotional turmoil and ambivalence underlying the mothers' help-seeking behaviours. Intersectionality therefore facilitated ways of knowing to capture the meanings mothers attached to their relationships with their children, husbands/partners, wider families, and communities for developing the concept of divided loyalties.

I turn now to a different study to illustrate another example of intersectional approaches to research.

Case study 2

Black Girls in the City Normalised Violence and Strategic Agency is a research project that examined how black girls and young women navigate their safety in the neighbourhoods they inhabit, which I undertook with my colleague Anna Carlile (Bernard and Carlile 2020). In this study, we sought to explore how black girls navigate the safety issues they have to contend with in public spaces and how they give voice to experiences of violence. To date, the lived experiences of young black women have not received much attention in the research. Utilising a qualitative approach, 18 young women between the ages of 14 and 19 were recruited from a youth club located in an inner-city local authority. The participants all self-identified as black British: seven black Caribbean, six black African, and five as mixed heritage (with one black African or Caribbean parent). The neighbourhood where the youth club is located suffers from material disadvantage such as poverty, high youth unemployment, and gang-related activities. All the young women lived in the immediate neighbourhood surrounding the youth club.

Data collection procedures utilised Photovoice techniques and focus group discussions guided by semi-structured interviews. Photovoice is a photographic documentary methodology that enables participants to represent their experiences through photographs and narrative (Wang and Burris 1997). Photovoice is an effective research method to elicit the voices of marginalised young people who are vulnerable, and it can bring lesser heard voices into research (Woodgate et al. 2017). In the focus group, the photographs were used to stimulate discussion about how the young women understood their safety needs. Data analysis was guided by some of the procedures from thematic analysis (Braun and Clarke 2006). Employing an intersectional lens provided the contextual framing to examine how the young women utilised their agency to navigate their physical environments.

As these young women belong to multiple oppressed groups because of their race, social class, gender, and age, we wanted to capture how systemic disadvantages create the conditions that heightens their risk to gender-based violence in public spaces. Against this backdrop, an intersectional framework helped with the critical engagement of some key questions for making visible the unseen, notably, the complex and simultaneous oppressions that their lived experiences are grounded in. Crucially, as a methodological tool, intersectionality allowed for close reading of the multifaceted nature of their daily efforts to navigate unsafe spaces in their neighbourhoods. In doing so, intersectionality helped us to uncover the layers of oppression that come together to shape and influence the young women's sense of agency and the nuances of how they exposed their vulnerabilities, that were often hidden behind a mask of toughness (hooks 1989). In this sense, then, intersectionality facilitated a nuanced understanding of the many layers of complexities of the physical and emotional labour they have to perform to navigate threats of sexual violence. Thus, intersectionality as an interpretive lens offered a way to explore the young women's sense-making to better understand their strategies of resilience and resistance. It is important to note here that one of the consistent threads that ran through the young women's narratives was the normalisation of the physical, emotional, and sexual violence they experienced. The key point to stress here is that intersectionality assisted us to interpret the data to be fully cognisant of the ways in which their circumstances and environments will shape and influence their coping mechanisms to illuminate how the young women's experiences are overlayed with trauma. As such, employing an intersectional approach offered the critical tools to help us conceptualise how the young women's experiences are constructed (Hill Collins and Bilge 2016). Furthermore, intersectional thinking enabled a better understanding of their narratives regarding what sustained the young women through their experiences. What is clear is that applying an intersectional frame of analysis to the young women's narratives allowed for a deeper engagement with the data to understand the coping strategies that buffer the harmful effects of trauma in their lives. Crucially, intersectionality helped amplify the voices of the young black women to foreground a key message to professional helpers, namely the importance of professional curiosity about the circumstances of black children in need of support and protection (Bernard 2019).

Reflective question

- What can we learn from intersectionality as an analytical concept for developing research that is sensitive to perspectives and lived experiences based on, for example, disability, race, age, gender, sexuality, and class?

Intersectional reflexivity

It is important to stress that the above examples are illustrative rather than exhaustive, helping to illustrate some of the ways that these two empirical research studies reflect an intersectionality perspective. In so doing, I have tried to demonstrate how intersectionality afforded me methodological choices to shape the research questions and develop analyses that are grounded in a clear feminist orientation. Most importantly, because my starting point was from a perspective at the intersection of feminism and anti-racism, employing intersectionality enabled me to broadly conceptualise and understand the complexities posed for black women and girls. In essence, in both studies I was able to use the concept of intersectionality as a framework to guide the research design and practices (Bowleg 2008; Windsong 2018). As well as posing questions directly about race and gender as simultaneous identities, intersectionality allowed me to elicit the salient factors that shape the research participants' experiences for the development of the emergent themes in the data for understanding the multi-layered situation of their problems (Bernard and Carlile 2020; Bernard 2013; Bernard 2001). In this regard, using key ideas of intersectionality such as inequality, social context, relationality, and complexity (Hill Collins and Bilge 2016), provides some ways to unravel the intersectional experiences to gain contextual understanding. Therefore, intersectional approaches opened up new approaches for a more comprehensive understanding of the interconnectivity of race, gender, age, and social class that significantly impacted the difficulties the girls and women in the research experienced.

It is worth bearing in mind that as a reflexive researcher, an intersectional methodology enabled me to understand my respective location in relation to the topic of intersectionality in qualitative research, and to recognise the limitations of the analysis that I constructed in both studies. Crucially, this highlighted the importance of paying careful attention to my own intersectional positionality which influenced my research topics, as well as the particular theoretical standpoint that I adopted to investigate these topics (Bernard 2017; Jacobson and Mustafa 2019). Here I am reminded of Alvesson and

Sköldberg's (2000) call for reflexive researchers to make transparent how their researcher's lens influences the interpretation of research participants' meanings, explanations, and experiences. Atewologun and Ramaswami (2018) similarly explored intersectional reflexivity to examine the ways that their lens of interpretation requires reflexive attention to their own social location, biases, and privileges throughout the research process.

Conclusion

This chapter has outlined some of the ways that intersectionality can be employed in research where multiple systems of oppression and structures of power are being explored. In my application of an intersectional framework to social work research, I demonstrated through two case studies how intersectionality can be used as an interpretive lens to analyse and theorise data and to explore the interplay of race, gender, and class, and that within this framing, we can better conceptualise and understand experiences that are complex and multi-layered. Although intersectionality has variously been criticised for not having an established step-by-step technique, nonetheless, I argue that an intersectional approach allows us to ask new questions about marginalised voices and experiences, and to critically engage with the everyday experiences of service users belonging to marginalised groups. In essence, the concept of intersectionality is valuable for social work research because it provides a means for analysing data in ways that enable a more nuanced understanding of everyday experiences that are significantly impacted by systemic inequalities (Bernard 2019). More significantly, an intersectional positioning provides opportunities to engage critically with an anti-oppressive approach to social work research, as well as for a deeper engagement with social justice values and ideals in practice. As such, I have argued throughout this chapter that intersectional ideas can provide directions in research to capture the intersection of social work research with social work values. For these reasons, intersectional analysis opens up possibilities in research to consider multiple sites of oppression for the development of knowledge that help to make sense of the complex problems social workers have to respond to in their practice.

References

Abrams, Jasmine A., Ariella Tabaac, Sarah Jung, and Nicole M. Else-Quest. 2020. Considerations for employing intersectionality in qualitative health research. *Social Science and Medicine* 258: 113–138.

Alvesson, Mats, and Kal Sköldberg. 2000. *Reflexive Methodology: New Vistas for Qualitative Research.* London: Sage.

Atewologun, Doyin, and Ramaswami Mahalingam. 2018. Intersectionality as a methodological tool in qualitative equality, diversity and inclusion research. In *Handbook of Research Methods in Diversity Management,* eds. Lize A. E. Booysen, Regina Bendl, and J. K. Pringle, 149–170. Cheltenham: Edward Elgar.

Bailey, Jane, Valerie Steeves, Jacquelyn Burkell, Leslie Regan Shade, Rakhi Ruparelia, and Priscilla Regan. 2019. Getting at equality: Research methods informed by the lessons of intersectionality. *International Journal of Qualitative Methods* 18: 1–13.

Bauer, Greta R. and Ayden I. Scheim. 2019. Advancing quantitative intersectionality research methods: Intracategorical and intercategorical approaches to shred and different constructs. *Social Science & Medicine* 226: 260–262.

Bernard, Claudia 2001. *Constructing Lived Experiences: Representations of Black Mothers in Child Sexual Abuse Discourses.* Aldershot: Ashgate.

Bernard, Claudia. 2013. Ethical issues in researching black teenage mothers with harmful childhood histories: Marginal voices. *Ethics and Social Welfare* 7 (1): 54–73.

Bernard, Claudia. 2017. Reflecting on a journey: Positionality, marginality and the outsider-within. In *Inside the Ivory Tower: Narratives of Women of Colour Surviving and Thriving in British Academia,* eds. Deborah Gabriel and Shirley Ann Tate, 88–90. London: Trentham Books.

Bernard, Claudia. 2019. Using an intersectional lens to examine the child sexual exploitation of black adolescents. In *Child Sexual*

Exploitation: Why Theory Matters, ed. Jenny Pearce, 193–207. Bristol: Policy Press.

Bernard, Claudia, and Anna Carlile. 2020. Black girls navigate the physical and emotional landscape of the neighbourhood: Normalized violence and strategic agency. *Qualitative Social Work*. sagepub. com/journals-permissions DOI: 10.1177/1473325020920341.

Blakemore, Tamara, and Amanda Howard. 2015. Engaging undergraduate social work students in research through experience-based learning. *Social Work Education* 34 (7): 861–880.

Bowleg, Linda, 2008. When black + lesbian + woman ≠ black lesbian woman: The methodological challenges of qualitative and quantitative intersectionality research. *Sex Roles* 59: 312–325.

Bowleg, Linda, and Greta Bauer. 2016. Invited reflection: Quantifying intersectionality. *Psychology and Women Quarterly* 40 (3): 337–341.

Braun, Virgina and Victoria Clarke. 2006. Using thematic analysis in psychology. *Qualitative Research in Psychology* 3 (2): 77–101.

Brotman, Shari, Ilyan Ferrer and Sharon Koehn. 2020. Situating the life story narratives of aging immigrants within a structural context: the intersectional life course perspective as research praxis. *Qualitative Research* 20 (4): 465–484.

Butler, Ian. 2002. Critical commentary: A code of ethics for social work and social care research. *British Journal of Social Work* 32 (2): 239–248.

Cameron, Pamela J., and David C. Este. 2008. Engaging students in social work research education. *Social Work Education* 27 (4): 390–406.

Case, Kim A. 2017. *Intersectional Pedagogy: Complicating Identity and Social Justice*. New York: Routledge.

Charmaz, Kathy. 1995. Grounded theory. In *Rethinking Methods in Psychology*, eds. Jonathan A. Smith, Rom Harré, and Luk Van Langenhove, 27–49. London: Sage.

Cho, Sumi, Kimberlé Williams Crenshaw, and Leslie McCall. 2013. Toward a field of intersectionality studies: Theory, applications, and praxis. *Signs* 38 (4): 785–810.

Choo, Hae Yoon, and Myra Marx Ferree. 2010. Practicing intersectionality in sociological research: A critical analysis of inclusions, interactions, and institutions in the study of inequalities. *Sociological Theory* 28 (2): 129–149.

Clarke, Averil Y., and Leslie McCall. 2013. Intersectionality and social explanation in social science research. *Du Bois Review* 10 (2): 349–363.

Cole, Elizabeth R. 2009. Intersectionality and research in psychology. *American Psychologist* 64 (3): 170–180.

Codiroli Mcmaster, Natasha, and Rose Cook. 2019. The contribution of intersectionality to quantitative research into educational inequalities. *Review of Education* 7 (2): 271–292.

Davis, Kathy. 2008. Intersectionality a buzzword: A sociology of science perspectives on what makes a feminist theory successful. *Feminist Theory* 9 (1): 67–86.

Department for Education. 2018. *Knowledge and Skills Statement for Child and Family Practitioner*s. London: HMSO.

Drummond, J. D., and Shari Brotman. 2014. Intersecting and embodied identities: A Queer woman's experience of disability and sexuality. *Sexuality and Disability* 32: 533–549.

Einbinder, Susan Dana. 2014. Reducing research anxiety among MSW students. *Journal of Teaching in Social Work* 34 (1): 2–16.

Else-Quest, Nicole M., and Janet Shibley Hyde. 2016. Intersectionality in quantitative psychological research: II. Methods and techniques. *Psychology of Women Quarterly* 40 (3): 319–336.

Ferguson, Iain, Vasilios Loakimidis and Michael Lavalette. 2018. *Global Social Work in a Political Context: Radical Perspectives*. Bristol: Policy Press.

Fish, Julie. 2015. Investigating approaches to the teaching of research on undergraduate social work programmes: A research note. *British Journal of Social Work* 45 (3): 1060–1067.

Fisher, Mike, and Peter Marsh. 2003. Social work research and the 2001 Research Assessment Exercise: An initial overview. *Social Work Education* 22 (1): 71–80.

Fehrenbacher, Anne E., and Dhara Patel. 2020. Translating the theory of intersectionality into quantitative and mixed methods for empirical gender transformative research on health. *Culture, Health and Sexuality* 22 (sup 1): 145–160.

Grace, Daniel. 2014. Intersectionality-informed mixed method research: A primer. *Health Sociology Review* 19 (4): 478–490.

Hardwick, Louise, and Aiden Worsley. 2011. *Doing Social Work Research.* London: Sage.

Hill Collins, Patricia, and Sirma Bilge. 2016. *Intersectionality.* Hoboken: Wiley.

Hillsburg, Heather. 2013. Towards a methodology of intersectionality: An axiom-based approach. *Atlantis* 36 (1): 3–11.

hooks, bell. 1989. *Talking Back: Thinking Feminist, Thinking Black.* Boston: Sheba Feminist Publishers.

Hulko, Wendy. 2004. Social science perspectives of dementia research: Intersectionality. In *Dementia and Social Inclusion: Marginalised Groups and Marginalised Areas of Care in Dementia Research, Policy and Practice*, eds. Anthea Innes, Carole Archibald, and Charlie Murphy, 237–254. London: Jessica Kingsley.

Hulko, Wendy, and Jessica Hovanes. 2018. Intersectionality in the lives of LGBTQ youth: Identifying as LGBTQ and finding community in small cities and rural towns. *Journal of Homosexuality* 65 (4): 427–455.

Humphries, Beth. 2008. *Social Work Research for Social Justice.* Basingstoke: Palgrave Macmillan.

IFSW (International Federation of Social Workers). 2014. Global agenda for social work and social development: First report: Promoting social and economic equalities. *International Social Work* 57 (4): 3–16.

Jacobson, Danielle, and Nida Mustafa. 2019. Social identity map: A reflexivity tool for practicing explicit positionality in critical qualitative research. *International Journal of Qualitative Research* 18: 1–12.

Kiik, Riina. 2005. The Estonian experience: How to inspire social work students to undertake research? *European Journal of Social Work* 8 (3): 329–334.

Krumer-Nevo, Michal, and Michal Komem. 2013. Intersectionality and critical social work with girls: Theory and practice. *British Journal of Social Work* 45 (4): 1190–1206.

Lyons, Karen. 2000. The place of research in social work education. *British Journal of Social Work* 30 (4): 433–47.

McCall, Leslie. 2005. The complexity of intersectionality. *Signs* 30 (3): 1771–1880.

Murphy, Yvette, Valerie Hunt, Anna M. Zajicek, Adele N. Norris, and Leah Hamilton. 2009. *Incorporating Intersectionality in Social Work Practice, Research, Policy and Education*. Washington DC: NASW Press.

Naples, Nancy A. 2009. Teaching intersectionality intersectionality. *International Feminist Journal of Politics* 11 (4): 566–577.

Rice, Carla, Elisabeth Harrison, and May Friedman. 2019. Doing justice to intersectionality in Research. *Cultural Studies: Critical Methodologies* 19 (6): 409–420.

Sharland, Elaine, and Barbra Teater. 2016. Research teaching and learning in qualifying social work education. In *The Routledge International Handbook of Social Work Education*, eds. Imogen Taylor, Marion Bogo, Michelle Lefevre, and Barbra Teater, 144–156. Abingdon and New York: Routledge.

Shaw, Ian F. 2007. Is social work research distinctive? *Social Work Education* 26 (7): 659–669.

Smith, Roger. 2009. *Doing Social Work Research*. Maidenhead: Open University Press.

Strauss, A. and Corbin, J. (1998) *Basics of Qualitative Research: Techniques and Procedures for Developing Grounded Theory*. Thousand Oaks, CA: Sage.

Syed, Moin. 2010. Disciplinarity and methodology in intersectionality theory and research. *American Psychologist* 65 (1): 61–62.

Teater, Barbra, Jessica Roy, John Carpenter, Donald Forrester, John Devaney, and Jonathan Scourfield. 2017. Making social work count: A curriculum innovation to teach quantitative research methods and statistical analysis to undergraduate social work students in the United Kingdom. *Journal of Teaching in Social Work* 37 (5): 422–437.

Teater, Barbra, John Devaney, Donald Forrester, Jonathan Scourfield, and John Carpenter. 2017. *Quantitative Research Methods for Social Work: Making Social Work Count*. London: Palgrave Macmillan.

Wang, C. and Burris, M. A. 1997. Photovoice: Concept, methodology, and use for participatory needs assessment. *Health Education and Behavior* 24 (3): 369–387.

Warner, Leah R. 2008. A best practices guide to intersectional approaches in psychological research. *Sex Roles* 59 (5–6): 454–463.

Whittaker, Andrew. 2012. *Research Skills for Social Work*. London: Sage/Learning Matters.

Windsong, Elena A. 2018. Incorporating intersectionality into research design: An example using qualitative interviews. *International Journal of Social Research Methodology* 21 (2): 135–147.

Woodgate, Roberta Lynn. David Shiyokha Busolo, Maryanne Crockett, Ruth Anne Dean, Miriam R. Amaladas and Pierre J. Plourde. 2017. A qualitative study on African immigrant and refugee families' experiences of accessing primary health care services in Manitoba, Canada: It's not easy! *International Journal for Equity in Health*. 16 (5): Published online 9 January 2017. doi:10.1186/s12939-016-0510-x.

8 Concluding thoughts

In this book, I weave together theoretical discussion, real-life case vignettes, and reflective exercises to explore applications of intersectionality to social work practice. Taking as my point of departure the notion that intersectional scholarship is crucially important for social work practice, the book emphasises the need to develop critical thinking about contexts of oppression, such as racism, sexism, ageism, ableism, disablism, and hetrosexism. Indeed, as I have suggested, there is a responsibility in social work to link private troubles to broader structures in order to address the root causes of the social problems that bring individuals and families from marginal positions to the attention of social welfare agencies. Thus, the chapters that comprise this book build the case for intersectionality as a lens through which we can analyse lived experiences in the context of social work practice. More broadly, using intersectionality as a starting point raises some fundamental questions about the role of power, privilege and experiences of discrimination and inequalities, for grounding understandings of such lived experiences. In this regard, this book will deepen understandings of the intersectional dynamics of oppression and inequalities that characterise the lives of service users who experience multiple layers of vulnerabilities.

A thread running through the book is that intersectionality as an analytical framework challenges social workers to take account of experiences impacted by social disadvantage. A strong line of argument is made that the principles of intersectionality align very closely with social work's core values, thus making it a key tool for social workers to understand how discrimination and oppression impact the lives of service users. As I have argued throughout the book, I want the reader to grasp that intersectionality provides a critical vantage point from which to develop practice that is grounded in awareness of the wider environmental factors that influence needs and vulnerabilities. The central

DOI: 10.4324/9780429467288-8

task of this book has been to introduce students and social workers to how an intersectional framework can enable more nuanced under-standings of the lives of people who are disproportionately impacted by social inequalities; the discussion therefore points to ways multiple dimensions of oppression can be made sense of using intersectional approaches. For example, as illustrated in chapters three to seven, an intersectional theoretical framework can be applied to a wide range of practice contexts for interrogating how intersecting dimensions of oppression add layers of complexities to the lived experiences of service users with marginalised status. To this end, the book's main argument is that the structural inequalities and resulting disadvan-tages experienced by minoritised groups create a particular context that increases vulnerability and risk. Therefore, through the lens of intersectionality, the contextual factors that have an impact on service users' lives can be approached with critical awareness.

Overall, the chapters bring together various strands to illuminate the workings of power and oppression, and, most notably, to pro-vide contextual understandings of the issues arising for oppressed people. I hope it has become clear that intersectionality can help us to gain a fuller understanding of experiences intermeshed in multiple minority identities. At its broadest level, the book seeks to show that intersectional approaches provide us with the possibilities to develop critical reflexivity for becoming comfortable with that which is inher-ently uncomfortable. Given the racially and ethnically diverse service-user groups that social work intervenes with, the employment of an intersectional approach offers essential tools for engagement with structures of oppression that shape their everyday lives (Bernard 2019). Essentially, practice that is rooted in intersectionality can cen-tre professional curiosity for thinking outside the box, which is neces-sary for engaging in reflective inquiry and dialogues that are about challenging uncomfortable truths. In other words, engaging intersec-tionality as an analytical framework can equip social workers with the tools of analysis that are necessary for navigating the complexi-ties and challenges that arise in practice. Special attention has been paid to the constantly shifting context of practice, to explore emerg-ing forms of practice issues being brought about by the changing racial and ethnic diversity of the populations that social workers must engage with. In essence, intersectional theory offers an alternative analytical framework for understanding how individuals, families, and groups may come to experience particular kinds of vulnerabilities during social work interventions.

Another theme that runs through the book is that, as social workers will repeatedly be brought face-to-face with the adverse consequences of structural inequalities, intersectional thinking helps to stimulate debates about the structural causes of the problems and issues that arise for those needing social work support. The arguments in the book call us back to the International Social Work Federation's reminder that social workers are engaging every day with life at its extremes, witnessing the highs and lows of human capabilities and behaviour (IFSW 2014). Hence, it is important to uncover the interlocking systems of oppression for developing approaches to practice that are rooted in social justice values and principles. In this sense, having the tools for critical engagement with the interconnected systems of oppression, alongside an acute awareness of our own positionality, is key to promoting diversity, equality, and social justice in social work. More specifically, however, a social justice perspective is an important tool for transformative social work practice, especially one that can interrogate the role of social work in particular when working with the marginalised and oppressed.

As I describe in the introduction, intersectional thinking has been used in various ways to develop liberatory pedagogy for learning for social work practice. In Chapter 6, I discussed at length how an intersectional pedagogy can open up a space for engaging new ways of thinking about complex lived experiences that are deeply mired in systems of oppression. In thinking about learning and teaching, I considered an intersectional pedagogical model to suggest strategies that can be used for anti-oppressive practice. In particular, I set out some of the ways that intersectionality can be employed to develop critical pedagogy for learning about power, oppression, and privilege. Indeed, I have introduced the intersectionality wheel and an intersectional pedagogy model to offer powerful tools for fostering participatory learning classrooms. Recognising an intersectional perspective offers some powerful conceptual and analytical tools for enabling difficult conversations to take place about different forms of oppressions. This book has therefore explored intersectionality as a theoretical frame to open up academic spaces for anti-oppressive teaching and learning. Intersectionality provides us with a way to understand the diverse experiences of people with multiple intersecting identities. Through such lens, the capacity to decipher the deficit discourse can counter Eurocentric ideas and beliefs that still underpin much social work theory and practice. Perhaps most importantly, intersectionality can enable the interrogation of the social work knowledge base for disrupting dominant claims about knowledge creation. Thus, at the heart of this book is the invitation to employ an intersectional approach to understand the lives of service users who are positioned at the intersection of multiple identity categories.

As social work is an applied discipline, intersectionality provides us with a conceptual frame to view the coming together of multiple identity markers in social work research. Of particular concern is to develop intersectional research to expand understandings of how experiences and identities converge for multiply marginalised groups. I have suggested that when used as a theoretical framework in research, intersectionality influences the questions we ask about experiences, and helps us to see the ways in which experiences are understood. In Chapter 8, as well as drawing on examples from my own work to show how I have used an intersectional framework in empirical research, I have also shared examples from a host of intersectional researchers to illuminate issues of race, gender, and class in research to deepen understandings of the nuances of lived experiences. A core concern here was to explore research that places the complex intertwining forms of oppression at the centre of its analysis in order to offer insights into the coalescence of factors that shape the everyday experiences of marginalised groups. The intention is to foster a more nuanced recognition of the factors that might hinder effective engagement in social work practice interventions with oppressed groups. In sum, the main project of this book is to show how intersectionality can be applied so as to better engage with the many forms of structural inequalities that shape the lived experiences of marginalised groups. These issues have significant implications for social work practice and the explorations provided in this book therefore offer alternative constructions and opportunities to stimulate new areas of inquiry. Thus, this book will increase the potential to identify new agendas for research with groups positioned within multiple systems of oppression.

It is worth mentioning here that during the writing of the final stages of this book, two issues have been at the forefront of debates in social work, namely the global Covid-19 pandemic and the Black Lives Matter movement. Specifically, the Covid-19 pandemic has affected some of the most vulnerable people in our society. In the UK, people from black, Asian, and ethnic minority backgrounds are disproportionately experiencing Covid-19 in negatively adverse ways and are at higher risk of death from the virus (Aldridge et al. 2020; Mamluk et al. 2020). It has been suggested that the pandemic has not only exposed systemic racial inequalities but has also amplified socio-economic disparities that intersect with race, age, gender, and other categories. In particular, the mental health impact of Covid-19 has been highlighted as a particular concern and it is suggested that the mental health impact will be felt for years after the pandemic ends (Johnson et al. 2021). Social work is at the forefront of responding to families and individuals impacted by Covid-19, and a key message of the book is that intersectionality assists in bringing together social care and justice work. At the same time, the Black Lives Matter movement sparked global protests following the killing of George Floyd by police in the USA, thus shining a spotlight on systematic racism and drawing attention to the racially motivated violence and race-related stressors that seriously affect black and minority ethnic people. Taken together, Covid-19 and the Black Lives Matter movement have brought a renewed interest in social work's role in addressing racism and social injustices.

Given the present moment in our society, this book offers conceptual tools that practitioners can utilise to disrupt deficit thinking through critical questions, and to have bold conversations about practices that do not replicate and uphold structural inequalities. As I have tried to show in the book, intersectionality provides an ideal framework for social work because it forces practitioners to confront critical questions about the structural inequities that create the challenges and conditions that bring racially oppressed groups to the attention of social welfare agencies. Ultimately, intersectionality is a means to theorise and interrogate the ways we work with those who are at the intersection of race, disability, gender, class, sexual orientation, and age.

References

Aldridge, Robert W., Srinivasa Vittal Katikireddi, Rohini Mathur, Neha Pathak, Rachel Burns, Ellen B. Fragaszy, Anne M. Johnson, Delan Devakumar, Ibrahim Abubakar, and Andrew Hayward. 2020. Black, Asian and Minority Ethnic groups in England are at increased risk of death from COVID-19: Indirect standardisation of NHS mortality data. *Wellcome Open Research* 5 (88). https://doi.org/10.12688/wellcomeopenres.15922.2.

Bernard, Claudia. 2019. Using an intersectional lens to examine the child sexual exploitation of black adolescents. In *Child Sexual Exploitation: Why Theory Matters*, ed. Jenny Pearce, 193–207. Bristol: Policy Press.

hooks, bell. 1989. *Talking Back: Thinking Feminist, Thinking Black.* London: Sheba Feminist Publishing.

IFSW (International Federation of Social Workers). 2014. Global agenda for social work and social development: First report: promoting social and economic equalities. *International Social Work* 57 (4): 3–16.

Johnson, Paul, Robert Joyce, and Lucinda Platt. 2021. *The IFS Deaton Review of Inequalities: A New Year's Message.* London: IFS/Nuffield Foundation.

Mamluk, Loubaba, and Tim Jones. The impact of COVID-19 on black, Asian and minority ethnic communities. Bristol: National Institute for Health Research and Bristol University.

Index

Taylor & Francis Group
an **informa** business

Taylor & Francis eBooks

www.taylorfrancis.com

A single destination for eBooks from Taylor & Francis
with increased functionality and an improved user
experience to meet the needs of our customers.

90,000+ eBooks of award-winning academic content in
Humanities, Social Science, Science, Technology, Engineering,
and Medical written by a global network of editors and authors.

TAYLOR & FRANCIS EBOOKS OFFERS:

A streamlined
experience for
our library
customers

A single point
of discovery
for all of our
eBook content

Improved
search and
discovery of
content at both
book and
chapter level

REQUEST A FREE TRIAL
support@taylorfrancis.com

 **Routledge**
Taylor & Francis Group

 **CRC Press**
Taylor & Francis Group